"Understanding, responding to, a  ships can be complicated for teena Roberts breaks down the barri advice every teen needs. From e-... and dating, Roberts offers sage advice teens can relate to. Written for teens yet valuable for parents, this is a coffee table book to leave around your home in the event your teen needs guidance she is hesitant to seek from you. Confused? Frustrated? Overwhelmed? Afraid? Just ask Emily. Then *Express Yourself.*"

> — **Lynne Kenney, PsyD**, mom to two teens, pediatric
> psychologist, international speaker, and coauthor
> of *Bloom: 50 Things to Say, Think, and Do with
> Anxious, Angry, and Over-the-Top Kids*

"Emily Roberts's *Express Yourself* is the ideal combination of humor, real talk, and research from which every girl can benefit. This book reminds young women of their power and influence, all while providing tried and true strategies for how to be the happiest, healthiest, best versions of themselves. It's fun, practical, and most definitely worth the read."

> — **Lexie Kite, PhD**, codirector of Beauty
> Redefined Foundation

"*Express Yourself* is exactly what the confidence conversation needs. With its great communication tools, helpful and rewarding exercises, and abundant opportunities for self-reflection, this book offers teens the tools they need to tackle life and all the obstacles that come with it."

— **Jess Weiner**, author and self-esteem expert

"In short, *Express Yourself* is excellent. Roberts provides practical skills and assertiveness-building exercises for teen girls—an audience who so desperately needs more voices telling them how to effectively stand up for themselves and why it's important to do so. Any girl who reads this will walk away with new positive communication techniques to implement in her life."

— **Ami Kane, MPA**, development director at the
Girls Empowerment Network (GENaustin)

"*Express Yourself* feels like a conversation with someone who really gets you—that wise and compassionate friend whose advice is always on target. It serves as a road map for teens to learn to take up space with their voice. That is a concept society works very hard to get girls to unlearn, but thankfully Roberts created a phenomenal guide to keep them in the practice of speaking their truth. Parents and educators will find this book to be a wonderful resource for the girls they care about as they transition into outspoken, confident young women."

— **Melissa Atkins Wardy**, speaker, consultant,
business owner, and author of *Redefining Girly*

"Emily Roberts's *Express Yourself* nails the beauty and complexity of girl's world. This much-needed book is packed full of wisdom to help young women navigate and normalize their teen years with bravery and confidence."

> — **Julia V. Taylor**, MA, author of *The Body Image Workbook for Teens*, *Salvaging Sisterhood*, and *Perfectly You*, and coauthor of *G.I.R.L.S. (Girls in Real Life Situations)* and *The Bullying Workbook for Teens*

"Emily Roberts has created a manual that can be useful to every adolescent girl. This book fills a void for girls struggling to manage difficult interpersonal relationships, and provides essential strategies for improving these relationships, as well as managing emotions during the challenging transition of adolescence. This is a great resource for adolescents, as well as for parents and professionals."

> — **Dr. Drew Pinsky**

the *i*nstant help solutions series

Young people today need mental health resources more than ever. That's why New Harbinger created the **Instant Help Solutions Series** especially for teens. Written by leading psychologists, physicians, and professionals, these evidence-based self-help books offer practical tips and strategies for dealing with a variety of mental health issues and life challenges teens face, such as depression, anxiety, bullying, eating disorders, trauma, and self-esteem problems.

Studies have shown that young people who learn healthy coping skills early on are better able to navigate problems later in life. Engaging and easy-to-use, these books provide teens with the tools they need to thrive—at home, at school, and on into adulthood.

This series is part of the **New Harbinger Instant Help Books** imprint, founded by renowned child psychologist Lawrence Shapiro. For a complete list of books in this series, visit newharbinger.com.

express
yourself

a teen girl's guide
to **speaking up** and
being who you are

EMILY ROBERTS, MA, LPC

Instant Help Books
An Imprint of New Harbinger Publications, Inc.

Publisher's Note

Distributed in Canada by Raincoast Books

Copyright © 2015 by Emily Roberts
        Instant Help
        An Imprint of New Harbinger Publications, Inc.
        5674 Shattuck Avenue
        Oakland, CA 94609
        www.newharbinger.com

Cover design by Amy Shoup
Acquired by Melissa Kirk
Edited by Gretel Hakanson

Library of Congress Cataloging-in-Publication Data on file

FSC
www.fsc.org
MIX
Paper from
responsible sources
FSC® C011935

Printed in the United States of America

19   18   17

10   9   8   7   6   5   4

This book is for you, my dear. That's right, you the young woman, the one reading these words. The world needs you to speak up and shine with confidence, to share your voice, and to become who you are supposed to be. This book is for all the girls and young women I've worked with who have shared their stories (you know who you are), who have bravely asked for help, and who have allowed me to join them on their journey to develop confidence. Tatum Emory, Tinsley Elizabeth, Olivia Marie, Lelia Marie, Imani Jayden, and Jenna Brooke, may this book be your guide to the teen years to come.

Contents

Foreword

Being a teenager is hard. This isn't exactly earth-shattering news. I'm guessing you could write your own book about how challenging being a teenager truly is. Adolescence is a time of great change: physically, mentally, and emotionally. It is the time of life when the most change occurs, second only to infancy.

As a teen, there are many things pulling you in lots of directions. You have your parents asking you for one thing, your friends asking you for something else, and maybe you want something altogether different. With all of this confusion, you may not know what to do, what to say, or how to act. Add into this confusion all of your emotions, and it can feel like a recipe for disaster. The challenge, frequently, is figuring out how to handle it all so you feel empowered and confident, all the while building and maintaining your important relationships.

It is challenging to know what skills to use to be true to yourself and to speak your mind. You may be feeling rifts in your relationships with your friends, family, or other people in your life. If you had the skills to help you communicate and manage your emotions better, your relationships with yourself and others would improve, your ability to navigate the world would be better, and you would begin to feel more confident in yourself and within your life.

Learning how to slow down, take a minute, and determine what you want to do or say effectively and efficiently are the keys to feeling comfortable in your own skin and communicating with ease. When you learn these skills, you will be assertive, confident, and comfortable with yourself.

My excellent colleague Emily Roberts has been working with teens and young adults for over a decade. Many teens she works with see her more as a mentor than a therapist due to her compassionate stance and realistic voice. She understands the challenges faced by teens and has created an innovative, powerful approach to help you achieve your goals and feel your best. This book arrives at an amazing time. It highlights the challenges you face and will teach you how to navigate them confidently and assertively. The skills within this book promote empowerment, understanding, and strength. By incorporating these skills into your daily life, you will feel more confident and self-assured, in control of your emotions, and more comfortable speaking up in any situation.

—Jennifer L. Hartstein, PsyD
owner, Hartstein Psychological Services
contributor, NBC's *The Today Show*
author, *Princess Recovery: A How-To Guide to Raising Strong, Empowered Girls Who Can Create Their Own Happily Ever Afters*
self-esteem ambassador, Dove Real Beauty Campaign

Acknowledgments

This book would not have been possible without the love, support, and guidance from my supportive cast and crew who taught me how to be the director of my own life and believed in my dream to inspire and empower girls. We did it.

Mom, Dad, and Sara: You taught me to chase my dreams, even when they led me halfway across the country. You've supported my wild ideas and always encouraged me to think for myself. I am beyond grateful to have such a unique upbringing—I know you probably never thought I would say so, but it has helped me feel anything but ordinary. Thank you for your endless supply of love, incense, and supplements.

Nana and Grandma: You ladies have shown me what it means to be a strong woman. I am inspired by your stories and your love.

My New York Cast and Crew

Jen, my role model, mentor, and confidant: You have shown me what a mentor really is, and I aspire to be like you someday;

your advice and expertise is invaluable. Without you, I really wouldn't be here—you trusted my ideas, put up with my procrastination, and pushed me to get out of my comfort zone. You trained me, not just in DBT, but in finding my confidence.

My consultation team: Y'all are amazing—you've shown me what collaboration really means! Thank you for your guidance and support. Even on the toughest days, you helped me find the middle path.

Gabby Bernstein, my guru of guidance: You inspired me to spread my message with the world. You believed in my dream and encouraged me to keep writing. You taught me to trust myself, and, finally, to sit still and be guided. I am forever grateful.

Blair and Rebeca, my NYC family: Blair, you're my soul sister; thank you for manifesting with me and making our lives a reality. Without you, Milo, Max, and Lux, I would have been lost. You showed me that everything really does happen for a reason. I love you! Rebeca, from our dorm room days to our adult lives, you taught me to break out of my comfort zone and believed in me, even when I didn't believe in myself. Thank you, sister.

Caroline, Sarah P. D., Meghan A., and the Malkis: You have been my editing eyes, ears, and wise minds. Without your support, Gchat collaboration sessions, and amazing advice, I would be lost. I am so humbled by your unique talents and creativity.

Charles: Thank you for supporting my ideas and my psyche in a way I never knew was possible. I love you.

Milo: My furry child, you are an angel. You taught me how to play again. Your endless supply of energy, kisses, and talented tricks got me out of my head when it was a hectic place to be. I am so grateful for the love of a dog, especially you.

My Texas Cast and Crew

Lacey: Your pep talks were often blunt but always a blessing. You taught me how to be authentic and taught me what a true friend is—thank you for your guidance. Dustin: you and Lacey taught me to take life as it comes, and to make friends that accept you for you—I love you guys. Nixon and Sarah L., my soul sisters: You showed me what friendship is; you picked me up, pushed me, and never let me give up. I look forward to many more adventures with you beauties.

Sandy, Carolyn, Conley, Meredith, and Robin: You've shown up for me in ways I never imagined possible. Thank you for holding space for me and believing in my dreams.

Jane Flynn, my guide! You pushed me to follow my dreams and provided me with a friendship that therapists dream of. I admire you and can't wait to collaborate with you again soon. Dr. Sunny Lansdale: You believed in this young therapist, gave me a place to put my dreams into action, and taught me the skills to help myself and others. I am grateful for you and the faculty at St. Edward's University.

Pam and Cham, my other mothers: I am grateful each day when I get to work alongside you in helping families at Neurogistics. Your faith in me has allowed me to feel like and become the expert. I am humbled to have you in my life.

My California Cast and Crew

Susan: Without you, this book wouldn't exist. I am tremendously grateful for your guidance, grammar, and great ideas. You helped me find my voice and gave me the tools to make a difference in this world.

Melissa, Jess, Gretel, and Wendy: Thank you for helping me spread my message to the girls of the world. You showed me that miracles exist, and sometimes they are found in a publishing house. Alexis Jones and Emily Greener: You girls rock! You believed in this young therapist's ideas, encouraged me to write, and helped me find my voice and my platform. I Am That Girl was my first experience in the writing and editing world, and without you and your incredibly talented crew, I wouldn't know the power of women with a purpose—to collaborate and educate.

Introduction

Become The Director of Your Own Life

*Every word you say has power. There is no
such thing as a powerless word.*

— Marianne Williamson,
Miracle Thought Podcast

Wouldn't it be nice if there were a pause button for life—like an app on your phone that could stop everything for just a minute? You could gather your thoughts, figure out how to handle a situation, and take a deep breath before pressing play. Even better, it could give you advice on what to do or say. How cool would that be? Say you're with your friends and all of a sudden your crush comes walking up; you freeze, and your mind goes blank. What do you do? What if your parents are on your case about your grades, how do you get them to relax and let you figure things out without starting an argument?

Unfortunately, there is no magic app (yet) that can stop time or tell you what to do in these uncomfortable circumstances, but this book is the next best thing. It will be your guide for communicating assertively—with confidence and without fear. For years, others have told you what to do, but now it's time to be the director of your own life. Your parents may act as if they're still running the show, but they're not in the director's chair—you are. They aren't with you day in and day out, handling the complicated circumstances you face. Your friends and peers may influence your decisions, but they are really just your cast and crew—you're the one calling the shots. You have the power to speak up and say yes or no in any situation—your life is your movie; you hold the power for making it a smashing success or a serious drama. You've just got to learn the secrets to handling the behind-the-scenes drama and difficulties that arise on set. This book is your guide to directing the life you want.

Not only will you receive step-by-step instructions, but you'll also have tools to develop your confidence in a major way and scripts to help you practice feeling and being assertive. All of these things will help make you more comfortable in tricky situations and make it easier to figure out what to say or do. How awesome does that sound?

Can You Relate?

It isn't easy being a teenager. There are a lot of factors that add up, and they may make you feel as if you're losing your mind. You've got parents acting like they're in charge, and friends who are your BFF one minute and then barely talk to you the next—not to mention the pressure of getting to school on time and making a good impression. All of these things can make you feel like a hot mess! This book will help you handle the strange feelings, find the words to speak your mind, and feel more self-assured in any situation you encounter.

Can you relate to any of these situations? Take a second to think about how you'd react and respond.

* Your friends didn't invite you to a sleepover. You find out you're the only one who didn't get an invite when you see their party pics on social media. Do you stay silent or let them know how you feel?

* Two of your close friends are in a huge fight, and you're stuck in the middle. How do you stay friends with both of them without choosing sides or hurting someone's feelings?

* All of your friends are planning to skip class and go off campus for lunch. You really want to go, but you'd be grounded for life if your parents found out. What do you do?

* Out of nowhere your crush stops talking to you, ignores you in the hall, and doesn't respond to your texts. You don't know why, and now you feel totally confused and embarrassed. Do you ask what's up?

* You just got the lead in the school play. You're so excited, but your friends aren't. They are less talk-ative and start leaving you out of their weekend plans. You don't know what you did wrong, and it hurts—what do you do?

These situations are challenging for anyone. Assertiveness is the key to feeling confident in any situation. It gives you the ability to speak your mind, feel comfortable, and get what you need.

Even if you haven't experienced these exact situations, it's likely that you know someone who has or that you'll find yourself in similar situations at some point over the next few years. Being a teenager is tough! You have more emotions than ever before, and you're faced with new situations that no one has given you directions for. What's worse, you're surrounded by other teens struggling with the same stuff, so they may not be the best help.

As you're well aware, there is no Google search or class at school that tells you exactly how to handle the everyday drama that comes with being a teenager in today's world. Your parents may think they understand, but life was different for them—so any advice they give you could feel outdated. Your friends may act like they know it all, but then you see them making bad decisions—so how can you trust them? Where do you turn to figure out how to deal with these tricky situations? This book was created to teach you how. So many girls, just like you, didn't know where to go or whom to trust when faced with the challenges of being a teenager. They didn't have a guide to help them navigate through the drama-filled days and extreme emotions, but you do! The situations presented in the following chapters are based on real events, from girls your age. These tools and solutions worked for them and will work for you.

New Territory

It might help to get a better understanding of why assertiveness is so difficult. The teen years are about defining who you are and becoming more independent, while, at the same time, finding ways to fit in and feel accepted. Add in popularity contests, catty friends, and unpredictable schedules, and you may wish you were back in preschool rather than prepping for college. Sure you've seen movies or heard how others have said they've handled these things before, but that's them, not you. They are not in your unique situation or in your mind.

The more you know about what is really going on inside you, the more confident you will feel when handling new experiences. Parents and adults sometimes forget that your brain and body are constantly changing during this time, often making you feel like an alien in your own home. The truth is these major changes affect the way you interact with everyone—and how everyone reacts to you, too.

It can be annoying to hear that, as a teen, you've become more "emotional" or "hormonal"—but it's true. Your body and brain are changing. Adults expect you to adjust and act appropriately. But has anyone clued you in about how to deal with the overwhelming emotions? Probably not. Knowing that you're more sensitive doesn't mean you get a free pass to react emotionally or aggressively. Going on a texting tirade to your best friend about how rude she's been lately won't end well, and blaming your behavior on the biological changes you're experiencing isn't cool. But if you know that she is one of those girls who pushes your buttons, you can remain in control once you learn the tools to communicate confidently. Your urges are one thing; your choices are another.

You've probably also noticed that you're not the only one who's emotionally unsteady. Your friends may suddenly become dramatic or easily upset, your parents seem to have a shorter fuse, and even your teachers may get more frustrated than a situation seems to call for. So both you and your environment are increasingly complicated. Sounds like a setup for some serious communication mishaps.

Biological Facts

If you're feeling moodier or more sensitive than you used to, it's not a sign that you're out of your mind; it's a sign that you're normal! In your teen years, your brain and body are morphing into your adult self. These changes, which you have no control over, can be pretty uncomfortable. But it turns out that there are some pretty awesome benefits as well. Here are some of the facts:

* Your brain is growing and firing new connections rapidly, which means you're able to absorb more information at a faster rate than before.

* Parts of your brain aren't completely developed yet, which may make you more sensitive or emotional. Along with hormonal changes, science shows this combination may give rise to newly intense experiences of rage, anxiety, fear, aggression (at others and yourself), excitement, and sexual attraction.

* Your body is growing stronger every minute.

* Your body is adjusting to hormonal changes on a daily basis, and these adjustments affect you all the time, not just when you're feeling the effects of PMS. Hormones can have a big (and unpredictable) effect on your mood, making you happy one minute and sad or angry the next.

* Exhaustion, not laziness, is most likely what makes you want to sleep all day. The stress you feel on a daily basis, combined with those crazy hormones

and long days at school, may cause major fatigue and lack of motivation. It's ironic that the adults in your life recommend eight to ten hours of sleep—which you need—but make it impossible to obtain by waking you up at the crack of dawn and piling on the homework as if you have all night!

Challenges in Your Environment

As a teen, you are constantly encountering new situations without much life experience to guide you. One day your best friend is ditching you to hang out with someone else; the next day a teacher loses your homework and gives you a zero. It can feel like the whole world is against you at times. The adults in your life might expect you to know what to do in these situations, but how could you? They're all new to you—even if you've seen these situations on TV or heard about them from your friends, you've never experienced them for yourself. Here are some of the things that probably factor in to your stress:

* Other people can be challenging. It's difficult to assert yourself with another person when that person is powerful, feels threatened by you, or is simply unskilled at communication.

* Acceptance by your peers is extremely important, but fitting in doesn't happen easily. Being a teen means struggling with identity and self-image.

* Technology overload can be a huge stressor. The older you get, the more access you have to gadgets

and social media. These tools can be great for connecting with others, but they can also be challenging to manage. It may sometimes feel as if they're taking over your life.

* You're under a lot of pressure, academically and socially, as school gets more challenging, friendships get more complicated, and parents push you to "do your best"—whatever that means! Not to mention you're exposed to the alluring world of hooking up, having sex, and experimenting with drugs and alcohol. Your extracurricular activities demand a lot of your time, and your social life seems to be getting more complicated by the minute. What's worse, your parents and teachers expect you to handle it all perfectly!

All these experiences affect your ability to communicate. You may feel insecure or worried because in the past when you've tried to express yourself, it went terribly wrong. Maybe you made mistakes. Maybe you were embarrassed in front of friends. Whatever has happened in the past can cause anxiety and fear about what could happen in the present or in the future. This anxiety can absolutely crush your confidence and keep you from being an effective communicator. When you're anxious, you may try to avoid certain situations or you might get so worked up that your message gets lost in the emotion and isn't received clearly. Practicing the right skills will help you bypass those negative stories in your head and approach your next conversation feeling more empowered.

The Road to Adulthood

The desire to feel accepted isn't just a teenager thing—though many adults in your life may tell you it is. You've probably been trying to figure out how to fit in since kindergarten, and you know that cliques, mean behavior, and peer pressure started long before you hit the halls of high school. One of the reasons adults make such a big deal about these things when you're a teenager—and one of the reasons you may feel it's more important now—is because now more than ever the choices you make can have a real impact on your future.

As a teen, you have more access to the adult world. If you make a poor choice, chances are you'll pay for it later on, if not immediately. For example, giving in to friends who pressure you to skip class and accidentally missing a pop quiz as a result may seem minor. But that zero just moved your grade from a B to a C, which could affect you more than you think. Your GPA goes down; your parents are disappointed; all of these consequences could have been avoided. That's why it's so important to learn how to speak up and respect yourself in even the most difficult or tempting situations. Your future self will thank you for it.

Exercise: Assess Your Assertiveness

Think of this book as your personal mentor—a guide to knowing what to do, what to say, and how to act assertively and effectively in common teenage situations. Before we get to the solutions, it might help to get a better sense of the ways you assert yourself (or don't) in different situations.

The best way to start making changes and forming new habits is to first identify your strengths and weaknesses so you can focus on the areas that need work. Let's take a look at how assertive and confident you already are. For example, maybe it's easy for you to talk with your parents, but with your friends you're much less comfortable. Read the following scenarios and ask yourself how you think you would feel and why. Choose one of these answers, and follow it with your explanation:

a) I feel totally comfortable because…

b) I feel somewhat uncomfortable because…

c) I feel very nervous because…

Then in your journal (which you'll be keeping throughout your work with this book), write what you would say or do if you were in that situation.

Example: You're working on a class project, and it seems as if the leader is giving you all the work. How do you feel about confronting her?

I feel somewhat uncomfortable because I don't want her to get mad at me.

1. You are confused about what your teacher is lecturing about. How do you feel about raising your hand to ask a question?

2. You have hours of homework, and your friend won't stop texting you about the drama she is dealing with. How do you feel about texting her back and saying that you're busy?

3. Your parents are blaming you for something your little sister did. How do you feel about telling them they're wrong?

4. You are at a party and don't know very many people. How do you feel about starting a conversation with someone new?

5. You are trying to study for your finals in the library. The students at the table next to you are being super loud. How do you feel about asking them to quiet down?

6. Your parents are making you stay home on a Saturday night because your grades have gone down, but there's an event you really want to attend. How do you feel about trying to negotiate a compromise?

7. Your teacher makes an inappropriate comment about you in front of the whole class. How do you feel about staying after class to talk to him about it?

8. You want to ask a crush to hang out after school. How do you feel about extending an invitation?

9. Your best friend keeps breaking plans with you to hang out with her boyfriend instead. How do you feel about telling her how disappointed you are (or that it's not okay with you that she keeps changing plans)?

10. A friend keeps posting photos of you that are embarrassing. How do you feel about asking her to take them down and to be more considerate of your feelings from now on?

What do you notice about your responses? Which situations seemed easier to deal with, and which ones were more difficult? Were there scenarios for which you had no idea what to do or say? It takes a little bit of self-reflection and a lot of honesty to accept that you may not have all the answers, but that's the first step toward preparing for all the potentially problematic situations to come.

How to Get the Most from This Book

As you read this book, keep a pen and notebook or journal close by because, as you know from the previous exercise, you'll have opportunities throughout this book to answer questions and do some self-reflection. You can underline and highlight the information that hits home. The exercises in the following chapters will help you stay accountable and aware of your progress. These activities will also help your brain remember the skills that have proven effective for many girls your age. Each chapter has reflection questions to enhance your understanding of the techniques that will help you as you take on the role of director in your life. It's important to be truthful and honest with yourself when completing the exercises in each chapter. Don't forget that this is personal, meaning that your responses are intended for your eyes only. There are "Write Your Script" prompts throughout this book as well. Use your journal to practice writing scripts for the example scenarios, or for anything else in your life that you might need a script for.

Chapter 1 is an introduction to the basics of assertive communication, including tips and techniques. Many of these techniques are informed by the skills taught in dialectical behavior therapy (DBT), an approach developed and written about by Marsha Linehan, a psychologist and professor at the University of Washington.

It might be helpful to refer back to the information in the first chapter as you read chapters 2 through 7, which address typical teenage situations that can be troublesome for many girls: friends and frenemies, family frustrations, digital drama, peer pressure, and talking to important adults. As you're reading, you may find yourself thinking, *I've never been in that situation,* or *I don't think that will happen to me.* You may be right; not every girl will experience every situation in this book. But preparing ahead of time for all kinds of situations will mean that you'll be more confident and self-assured no matter what tight spot you find yourself in.

Each chapter has some awesome bonuses to inspire you and encourage you to speak up and shine. Throughout the book, inspirational quotes and the sections titled "Been There, Done That—Advice from Women Who've Been in Your Shoes" will show you how real women and girls communicated with confidence and changed their lives, as well as the world. If you find that these stories resonate with you, flip to the references section to find out more about these women and girls, and friend them on social media.

You can also stay connected with me, the Guidance Girl, and continue to build your confident communication skills. Feel free to e-mail questions to me at emily@theguidancegirl.com. You can follow me on Twitter (@GuidanceGirlEm) and become part of the Express Yourself movement, getting support and gaining friends using the hashtag #ExpressYourself; you can also follow me on other social media—on Instagram at @GuidanceGirlEm or my Facebook page, The Guidance Girl—or visit my website for daily doses of confidence at http://www .theguidancegirl.com.

Speaking of social media, if you've thumbed through the book already, you've likely noticed the hashtag messages within each chapter. These hashtag messages, called "Director's Notes," aren't there just because they're fun to use (you know they are!); they're messages that you can share on social media and use to connect with other girls and women who are becoming the directors of their own lives. How cool is that? Using the hashtag #ExpressYourself is about sharing the directing skills you're learning with the world, finding new friends and supporters of your new skills on your social media channels (Instagram, Twitter, Facebook, whatever you choose), and encouraging you to speak up, shine, and start directing the movie of your life.

By the time you turn the last page of this book, you'll be ready to handle just about any situation life throws your way. In your journey to adulthood, knowing how to let your emotions guide you—rather than control you—could make the difference between an awful and an awesome experience. Ready to get started? Turn the page to start learning the directing skills you'll need to take control of your life and communicate with confidence—but before you do, here's your first hashtag of inspiration.

Director's Note

When you speak up, you shine with confidence.

#ExpressYourself

Chapter 1

Communicating with Confidence

Write your own part. It is the only way I've gotten anywhere.
It is much harder work, but sometimes you have to take destiny
into your own hands. It forces you to think about what your
strengths really are, and once you find them, you can showcase
them, and no one can stop you.

— Mindy Kaling, *Why Is Everyone Hanging Out*
Without Me? (And Other Concerns)

The high school years are notoriously stressful. Every day brings new challenges—like asking a teacher for an extension on your essay, dealing with bossy friends, or trying to get your parents off your back. Do you ever wish you had a superpower that would make everything easier? I'm not talking about the ability to fly, read minds, or make yourself invisible. The power that would *really* be helpful is the ability to speak up and shine in any situation.

Assertiveness is the magic wand you've been looking for. It's the skill that will help you get along with people and get what you want. It'll help you express yourself when your crush doesn't text you back or your friends are talking behind your back. When you're assertive, you're showing others that you're comfortable in your own skin. And when they see that, they respect you. Even if you don't know exactly what to say or do, you appear (and feel) more assured and able to handle whatever situation the day brings.

Consider this scenario: Say your phone is about to die, and you've only just started the day. You want to borrow the charger that's on the desktop of the student sitting next to you. Asking if you could borrow it would be assertive. Reaching over and grabbing it would be aggressive. Which way would be more likely to make the other student feel comfortable in letting you borrow the charger?

Here's another example: You hit up your favorite coffee shop and order the usual, a mocha latte. When you take a sip, you realize it's the wrong drink. It's some green thing—gross! You might feel embarrassed to speak up and ask for what you ordered, or you may have the urge to respond with a snarky "Um, hello! Did you not see this drink is green?" or with sarcasm—"Nice job with the mocha latte!" But assertiveness is not about being rude. It's about saying what needs to be said nicely—in this case, something like, "Excuse me. I know you're busy, but I actually ordered a different drink. Could you please remake it for me? Thank you!"

Don't Be a Doormat

Now suppose you were to respond passively instead—walking off and drinking the green stuff anyway. Who would you be angry or frustrated with when you replayed the scene in your mind—maybe first at the barista who made the mistake? But after a few minutes, you would probably see that the blame is on you because you didn't speak up.

A passive response might seem easier in the moment, but it will likely lead to feeling disrespected and regretting staying silent. These kinds of feelings, even over a minor incident, will diminish your confidence rather than boost it, maybe leading you to overthink what you "should have" done, even though you can't do anything about it now. (And, let's be honest, replaying the scene in your head until you're exhausted is not the best way to use your free time!)

In other words, if you don't speak up because you're confusing assertiveness with aggressiveness, you risk being disrespected for a different reason. Those who are overinvested in being "nice" and are uncomfortable expressing their needs give others the message that they are insecure. If you're like this, people will see you as a doormat—someone who gets walked all over because you don't know what to say or you're afraid to say it. This is really common among girls and women—the fear that others will judge them or get mad at them if they speak up for themselves. But the more you let others walk all over you, the harder it becomes to be assertive—you accept less than you deserve, which becomes a habit, making it a challenge to be anything other than a doormat.

Director's Note

Be the director of your life, not a doormat. Act assertively.
Ask for what you need to avoid users and abusers.

#ExpressYourself

Assertiveness Is Not Aggressiveness

People sometimes confuse assertiveness with aggressiveness, but they're not the same thing at all. Being assertive means speaking your mind in a self-respecting way. Being aggressive means acting or reacting in a pushy, angry, or defensive way.

Think about the coffee shop situation. An aggressive person is likely to make a scene by yelling or being disrespectful to the barista. That comes across as rude, which is why it's so embarrassing to be around aggressive people, especially in public! Aggressiveness is not likely to make people respect you, and it's definitely not an effective way to get what you want. It might make for a more dramatic scene, and when you replay the scene later on, you will probably feel guilty, angry, or embarrassed by your behavior. These feelings don't lead to confidence. Also, aggressive communicators often hold in their real feelings, which then eat them up inside, leading to less self-confidence and more self-loathing.

Keep in mind that acting passive or aggressive isn't always done on purpose; in fact, it rarely is. Sometimes people just don't know what to do in new situations, especially when they feel disrespected. So they do what comes easily or what they've seen others do in similar situations. Like all communication skills, assertiveness is something that needs to be learned and practiced in order to get it right.

Be the Director of Your Own Life

Assertiveness is about saying what needs to be said and doing what needs to be done to make things happen. Again, think of it as being the director of your own life. If you were making a movie, you wouldn't want other people making all the decisions about the cast, the script, the costumes, the music, and the location—would you? And let's face it: as the director of your own life, you don't want your parents picking out your clothes or your friends choosing your prom date. You, the director, are the boss. And it's only right that you should have a say in the decisions.

As the director, you also get to choose your own role in the drama. Take a look at the following cast of characters. Which roles do you usually play? Which ones do your friends and family members play?

Exercise: Cast of Characters

The Avoider: Hates to argue and would rather hide out alone or with other friends until the air has cleared. Doesn't like to talk about her feelings. May respect herself but either doesn't know how to express herself or is afraid to, or both.

The Aggressor: Pushy, rude, demanding, unpleasant to be around. Hurts others, and rarely apologizes because she thinks she's always right.

The Passive-Aggressive: Expresses herself through side comments or silence, rather than confronting people directly. Expects others to pick up on her subtle cues and read her mind.

The Defender: Takes things personally and automatically resists a potentially helpful conversation. Can't seem to hear or respond to what others are saying about her without getting defensive.

The Drama Queen: Makes mountains out of molehills. Turns an everyday conflict into a big fight and broadcasts it to the whole world.

The Director, or Confident Communicator: Appears calm and sure of herself, and expresses her feelings and preferences without being demanding. Respects herself and those around her.

Directing Techniques

The role of a director isn't just to tell people what to do or say on the set of a film—it's an art. You've got to be creative and learn the skills to take the words on a page and bring them to life on screen. And you need to communicate with your cast and crew in ways that will make them listen to you and respect you. You don't have to do these things perfectly, of course, but you have to do them well. If you follow the techniques below, plus add a personal touch, you are bound be confident and in control.

These techniques will help you communicate with anyone, even the most stubborn, critical, and judgmental characters in your life. Think of these as tricks, like behind-the-scenes special effects that may be unbeknownst to the audience but have a huge impact on making your scene memorable—or, in this case, making your relationships with others a whole lot easier. When you know what to say and how to express it right, the people in your life will listen.

Take this scene, for example: Your BFF is livid because you ditched her after school to hang out with your crush. You didn't totally ditch her; she just never responded to your texts about changing plans, so you figured it was fine. You wish she would understand because you want to stay friends and not get into an epic argument.

The Art of Agreeing

This technique works behind the scenes to make a huge impact on your audience. Difficult people feed off of defensiveness, so one of the most powerful communication tricks is to get them to stop being so defensive by agreeing with them. Don't let the word "agreement" fool you—you don't have to admit fault if you haven't done anything wrong. You simply have to disarm those who are being defensive—meaning that you lessen the intensity of their emotions.

The idea of agreeing with someone who is pushing your buttons may be maddening, but the thing is, it's effective. It gets her to stop, focus on you, and chill out, diffusing the argument before it becomes a full-blown attack. You may be thinking, *How do I pretend to agree with her side when she is totally wrong?* Try this trick: Put yourself in her shoes for a second. Ask yourself why she's acting or reacting this way. Maybe your friend whom you ditched for your crush feels left out or is a little jealous, or maybe it's just that she really wanted to hang with you and was looking forward to it all day. Even if she's acting irrational, you can understand why she may be feeling this way.

What if your friend starts yelling at you the next day at school? Here are a few ways to disarm her using the art of agreeing:

* "You're right; that was really rude of me."

* "You have a right to be angry. I didn't think about your feelings, and I'm sorry about that."

* "I can understand why you're upset; that would have made me upset too."

She's shocked because you didn't argue, and she may even be a little confused, but the point is you successfully avoided an argument.

The Art of Expressing

Saying how you feel and what you need can be challenging and awkward—especially with pushy people. Before you say anything, there are some things you can do to prepare: pay mindful attention to what you are doing, determine how you are really feeling, and create a script. Having a script can help you be clear and confident and express what you really want to say.

Mindfulness means deliberately paying attention to whatever you are doing, right now. Try to focus for just a few minutes fully and completely on these warm-up exercises, and see if the intensity of your feelings around the situation is reduced afterward.

* Take a belly breath. Place your hand on your stomach, right below your belly button and notice if your belly is going in and out. Feel your hand rise about an inch each time you inhale and fall about an inch each time you exhale. Your chest will rise slightly. This is a real, true, deep breath. It sends oxygen to the brain and helps you get out of panic mode. Shallow breaths, or chest breaths, are what many of us tend to do when stressed or worried— but they only make you more anxious—oxygen is constricted, and your brain doesn't get fully fueled. Taking a few belly breaths helps your brain calm down and helps you make better decisions. When

you belly breathe, you're able to respond to stress assertively, not dramatically.

* Focus on your feet. That's right; notice your feet in your shoes (no one will notice you doing this), how your socks feel, and where you feel your shoes connected to your feet. Then move to your big toe. Can you wiggle it; how about your pinky toe? Now try it on your other foot.

* Count. Use your surroundings to count tiles on the floor, count the pictures in the room, or make up your own game using people around you. How many people are wearing hats, white shoes, or flip flops? If you don't want to use your environment, try counting back from one hundred by threes until you stump yourself.

* Listen to music mindfully. Pick a song with words and focus on lyrics or how many times the musician says a particular word such as "love." Or listen for the other instruments in the background, trying to focus on just one, such as the bass or drums.

When you are feeling mindful and able to understand how you are feeling, it's time to start thinking about your script.

What Are You Feeling?

Take a moment to recognize how you are feeling right now. Recognizing how you feel is the first step in controlling your emotions, which leads to expressing yourself effectively and confidently. Here are some words to help you express your emotions:

* Anger: frustrated, upset, angry, irritated, annoyed, mad, pissed, disappointed, hurt

* Scared: anxious, freaked out, worried, nervous, fearful, uneasy, weird

* Guilt: embarrassed, ashamed, disappointed, afraid, upset, bad

* Sad: hurt, depressed, lonely, hopeless, upset, uncomfortable, down

* Confident: excited, incredible, happy, capable, optimistic, amazing, awesome, great, hopeful

Creating Your Script

Here are five important steps to follow when creating your script.

1. Warm up. Before you head on the field for any sport or step on the stage to perform, you need to warm up your muscles and your mind. If your goal is to speak up and stay confident, your warm-up will help you get focused on that goal, not your fears. This warm-up might take just a few seconds, but it's super important in making sure you're in the zone—so your emotions aren't running the show, you are. Take a minute to breathe, do one of the mindfulness exercises above, or find a way to distract yourself to reduce the intensity of your feelings before saying a word. The more control you have over your emotions, the more confident you will feel.

2. Be mindful of your tone. Rehearse how you want it to sound in your head. Do you want to sound like an understanding and easygoing pal or a sarcastic mean girl ("Oh really, you're really yelling at me in front of everyone?")? Don't raise your voice, even if she does—that's just asking for a bigger explosion. Instead, focus on speaking slowly and respectfully. Ask yourself, "Would my teacher respect me if she walked by and saw how I'm interacting in this situation?" In other words, use a tone you'd be proud of.

3. Don't act out your feelings; keep control by expressing them in words, using "I feel" statements: "I feel nervous," "I get upset when I'm yelled at." Show the person you're speaking with that you have feelings, too. As simple as it sounds, hardly anyone does it right. When you say "I feel," it's like an emotional antenna, triggering empathy in the other person. "Hey, I'm really feeling upset about this because I didn't mean to hurt you" is way more powerful than "Don't be mad; it was a misunderstanding." Take the feeling words from the list above and create a few "I feel" statements of your own.

A quick tip: don't use the *f* word. Not *that f* word—try to avoid the word "fine." It's too neutral and usually indicates that you are anything but fine! Now, try practicing this kind of expression: Imagine that you are the friend who got ditched. How would you feel? Now, imagine that you are the friend who did the ditching. How would you feel?

4. Avoid "you" statements: "you're being too sensitive," or "you always get upset about these things." Instead, say, "I feel misunderstood," or "My intention wasn't to hurt you," which has a much different vibe. "You" statements start arguments because "you" automatically triggers a defensive response.

5. Ask for what you want or hope for, or state your goal for the conversation: "I really want to work this out," or "I want for us to understand each other better."

Director's Note

When in doubt, breathe it out.
Chill before you spill your guts or speak your mind.

#ExpressYourself

How to Write Your Script

In order to be confident in any situation and communicate clearly and effectively, it's necessary to have an understanding of the basics. Below are the steps to follow in almost any situation.

1. Identify your emotions.

When you're clear about what you're feeling, you'll speak with more confidence. You may have many different feelings, and that's fine. Just make sure that you're clear about what your emotions are telling you. Refer to the last "What Are You Feeling" box to help gain clarity and control.

2. Identify your goal.

Whether you are attempting to get the latte you ordered or trying to say no without starting an argument, in every situation there is a desired outcome. So before you speak your mind, clarify your goal. You may not know exactly what to say or how to say it, but if you know what you want, you can start there. What do you hope to gain from the situation with your BFF? It's likely that things can go back to normal and both of you can leave the situation feeling better. Even if the situation isn't as emotionally overwhelming, say talking to a teacher or asking for a few bucks from your parents—when you know what your goal is, it will help you remain confident in communicating.

In the situations that are addressed in the chapters that follow—and in most circumstances you encounter in your life—having one of the following goals in mind helps you create a "script" and stick to it.

* Building or maintaining a positive relationship.

* Staying close friends or on good terms with someone.

* Repairing a relationship after an argument or fight.

* Getting someone to listen to you or to do what you want or need.

* Maintaining your self-respect and your role as the director of your own life.

3. Set the scene.

Location is key, so be mindful of where you want to have this conversation. Confronting a friend about her crummy behavior is not likely to have a good outcome if done in the middle of the cafeteria or through text message. The best situations are ones that you have some control in, like taking a walk outside and talking with her privately. You'll have more confidence when you can speak face-to-face, and when you don't feel like an audience is watching.

4. Find the right time.

The saying is true: timing is everything. If you're in a rush, or the person you're trying to talk to is having a bad day, it may be a good idea to find a better time for the conversation, one that works for both of you.

5. Rehearse your script and stick to it.

Keep your main points in mind, and remember what you want the outcome to be. If you find you're getting flustered, take a moment to breathe, and then return to your script.

Write Your Script: What would your goal be in the argument with your BFF discussed earlier? Using the skills listed above, write the script for how you would handle it.

How to Appear Confident

You may be thinking, *how will I ever remember all these rules?* It can seem really overwhelming, which is why we will practice using them in different ways in each chapter. However, if you forget and freak out when you're faced with a new situation, here are a few basic points to remember that will help enhance your inner and outer confidence.

1. Let your body do the talking. Nonverbal communication —body language and facial expression—can be just as important as your words. Posture is key. Slouching and looking at the ground makes you look like a pushover (as if, literally, someone could push you over). Standing up straight reflects confidence.

2. Choose your tone of voice. A friendly or gentle tone of voice is helpful in any kind of confrontation. Stay away from sarcasm. Speak clearly—not loudly—if you want others to hear you, and be careful not to sound aggressive.

3. Be a good listener. How you listen is just as important as how you speak. Put down your phone, take out your earbuds, and try to focus on what is being said. Look directly at the person who's talking to you. Communicate respect with your facial expression—hold off on the frowning or eye rolling.

4. Be empathetic. Put yourself in the other person's shoes and imagine what she's feeling. Ask yourself how you would want to be treated if the roles were reversed.

5. Smile. If you aren't happy, don't try to fake it, but smiling generally lightens your mood and makes other people respond more positively to you.

Reflection Questions: If you were directing the earlier scene with your best friend, how would you explain the confident communicator role to your actress?

Want to take it a step further and get real with yourself? Go to the mirror and look at your facial expressions as you pretend to listen. What do you see: anger, disgust, shock? Notice the ways that your body language speaks louder than words.

The rest of the chapters in this book will help you apply these communication skills to various situations—with your friends, with your family, with your peer groups, with adults, and online. But first, it might be helpful to assess how comfortable you are communicating in different settings.

Exercise: How Comfortable Are You When Communicating with Others?

This questionnaire will help you identify strengths and weaknesses in your current style of communication. Get out your journal and answer the questions as honestly as you can. (The answers are for your eyes only!) The more specific your answers, the better, as they will help you become more aware of where you could use some improvement.

1. How do you feel about talking in class or speaking in public? Does it freak you out, or do you feel an exciting rush from expressing yourself in front of others?

2. When initiating conversations, do you tend to shy away from starting up a dialogue and wait for others to make the first move? Or do you dive in without hesitation, chatting it up with ease?

3. After a conversation or interaction, do you ever worry about how others perceived you? When you leave the situation, are you often plagued with thoughts about what you could have said differently or should have avoided, or the way you acted?

4. Are there particular people you feel totally comfortable with? Who are these people, and why do you think you feel this way around them?

5. Are there people in your life whom you feel nervous or uncomfortable around? Perhaps you notice feeling fake, like you have to pretend or put on a "mask" of your real self. Do you notice feelings of anxiety or nervousness when you are around them? Who are these people, and why do you think you feel this way?

6. Are there places or situations that you actively avoid? What makes them difficult for you and why do you think they stress you out?

7. When talking to others, do you ever get tense muscles or butterflies in your stomach or feel like your heart's beating out of your chest? Which people or situations make your body feel funny?

8. Do you ever avoid situations due to the fear of not knowing what to say or do? What situations have you avoided?

What did you learn from this exercise? After you've read the rest of this book, you might want to go back and revisit these situations with new ideas about how you could do things differently to make yourself more comfortable and more effective in each circumstance. In the meantime, let's move on to the particular complications of our first topic: friends and frenemies.

Director's Note

Difficult people are defensive. Confident people put themselves in others' shoes and attempt to understand.

#ExpressYourself

Chapter 2

Friends & Frenemies

All it takes is one girl who is brave enough to speak the truth to give others permission to do the same.

— Emily Greener, Cofounder and CEO, I Am That Girl

As you've grown up, you've experienced many different types of friendships. Some have grown into unbreakable bonds, while others have ended in fights or just faded away. Friendships are supposed to be fun and supportive, but they can also be one of the most frustrating parts of your life. Girls crave close bonds with each other, but all sorts of social realities get in the way. Communication can be tricky, and friendships can seem impossible to maintain—unless you have the right tools. By the end of this chapter, you should feel better equipped and more comfortable expressing yourself with friends.

Friend or Frenemy?

Good friendships are built on mutual respect and support. Frenemies, on the other hand, are enemies disguised as friends—people who put you down behind your back. A frenemy can be someone you've known for years or for just a few hours. No matter the length of time, at some point you realize your friendship with her makes you feel worse about yourself.

Exercise: Cast of Characters

Here's an exercise to get you thinking about the girls and guys in your life—which ones are friends and which are more like frenemies? Make a list (in your mind or in your journal) of the people you know who fit into the cast of characters below.

The Gossiper: The person who talks about others behind their backs and can't be trusted. She blabs about others and is probably doing the same to you.

The Confidant: The one you share your secrets with because you know she won't say a word to others. This person is also dependable and keeps her word.

The Antagonist: The person who likes to create and perpetuate drama by spreading rumors or spilling secrets.

The Cheerleader: A friend who's super supportive and tries to boost you up with kind words or silly texts. You can count on her for a smile when you're bragging about your achievements or a listening ear when you're down in the dumps.

The Downer: Someone who's pessimistic or negative, frequently talks about things that are depressing, and makes you feel drained. These energy suckers may not be aware of their melancholy mood. They ask for advice but never take it, leaving their friends feeling frustrated and helpless.

The Social Butterfly: The one who is always introducing friends to one another and wants them all to get along. She loves to connect with others and is easy to get along with.

The Social Climber: The person who tries to do whatever it takes to be popular, sometimes breaking plans with you when something "better" comes along. She's unreliable, but her intermittent attention keeps you from giving up on the friendship.

- Which of these people make you feel better about yourself, and which ones make you feel insecure?

- Which characters would you most likely form healthy friend-ships with?

- What about the characters who are more like frenemies—what makes them less likely to be true and trusted friends?

- Are there some people on your list who have switched roles? (Maybe in middle school they were "confidants," and now they seem more like "social climbers.") How does this change affect you?

- Which character do you most identify with? Is this the role you want to play?

Many girls, even grown women, have friends who are more like frenemies—so-called friends who make them anxious and keep them hanging by a thread. You know the type: the girl who gets mad at you when you haven't done anything wrong or the one you're too afraid to kick out of your life even though she doesn't treat you with respect. Maybe you feel the need to act like someone else just to fit in, or you ignore your self-respect to stay on this person's good side. Think that's acting as the director of your own life? Think again—being an impostor is far from feeling and acting confident.

So why do you put up with friends who continue to bully or belittle you? Why do people fall prey to such toxic relationships? For many, it's the fear of the unknown. Who will you hang with if not with them? What if you're not able to find better friends? But the truth is, the fewer toxic people in your life, the more self-respect and confidence you will maintain. (And by the way, self-respect and confidence are the perfect combination when it comes to attracting real friends!) The first step is to be aware of your rights in any friendship.

Director's Note

You deserve friends who make you happy, not ones
who make you feel crappy.

#ExpressYourself

Your Rights

* You have the right to nurturing and supportive friendships.

* You have the right to your own opinions and ideas.

* You have the right to say no in situations that make you uncomfortable.

* You have the right to feel safe and comfortable with your friends.

* You have the right to decide how you spend your time and which friendships you prioritize.

As you become more aware of the differences between friends and frenemies in your life, it's likely you'll want to make some changes. With both friends and frenemies, you'll find yourself facing many frustrating situations. Though you may not be able to change their behavior, the show must go on. It helps to have a script to follow, plus some practice with assertiveness skills, to keep from overreacting, obsessing, or getting stuck in a situation where you don't know what to do or say.

The situations presented in this chapter are ones that are frequently experienced by teenagers. They may not resemble the particular dilemmas you're dealing with, but these scripts can be adjusted to fit many different situations in which speaking up can be challenging. If a scenario doesn't seem to apply to you, it may at some point, so it's worth asking yourself, "What would I do if I were in this situation?" Having some ideas about how to handle it will increase your confidence—and your chances of success—in the future.

The Situation: The Teasing Isn't Funny

Sarah and I have been best friends for years. When we're alone, we have a blast. But when we're at school or with other friends, she's always teasing me. The other day she brought up an embarrassing story in front of my crush. I was mortified! She said I shouldn't be so sensitive, that it was just a joke. She's started to make fun of me online, too. The other day she commented on a picture of me and wrote, "Frizzy hair much? Looks like someone needs a hat! Yikes!

JK ;)." I don't know why she would think that's funny. She knows I hate my hair. How do I get her to stop teasing me once and for all?

Not all teasing is terrible. It can be a way for friends to connect, share humor, and break tension. Saying "You're such a nerd," for example, is probably more playful than hurtful, especially when it's delivered with a genuine smile, from one proudly geeky girl to another. If she really means it in a friendly way, her tone will be casual. And if it turns out that she (unintentionally) hurt your feelings, she'll be apologetic. When it's a dig, on the other hand, your hurt feelings will be met with defensiveness, as in "Chill out—it was just a joke!"

When friends look for ways to make you feel embarrassed or insecure, that's going beyond fun; they're trying to get under your skin. If your friend says, "OMG, your face gets bright red when your crush is around! Looks like someone is in love!" she may not actually be trying to upset you, but her fun is at your expense. She's joking *at* you, rather than *with* you.

Words can be powerful weapons. Continuing to tease or put someone down when the person appears hurt is an example of taunting, which is a form of bullying. Deliberately trying to make someone uncomfortable is just plain mean. (A good rule of thumb is this: if you wouldn't want a teacher to overhear your comment to a friend, you probably shouldn't say it out loud.)

Before You Say a Word

You might want to look back at chapter 1 and review the steps to take before approaching your friend. Here are the key steps:

1. Identify your goal. Are you trying to get your friend to hear you? To treat you differently?

2. Identify your emotions and their intensity. Are you more frustrated or hurt? Angry or upset? Find the right words to describe how you're feeling.

Set the Scene

Where and when is this scene going to be shot? In the cafeteria, in front of all your friends? Or at a quiet table in the courtyard after school? Do you want to wait until you've settled down or do it in the moment? If possible, ask her to meet you outside right after the conflict occurs, so it's fresh in your mind and hers. The longer you put it off, the more worried and anxious you'll feel. Approaching her in a demanding or aggressive way—"We need to talk, now!" —sets the stage for a fight. Instead, try a less dramatic approach: "Hey, can you come outside with me for a minute?"

What to Say

"Writing the script" is often the hardest part. So here's an acronym you can use when you're at a loss for words: *HEARD*.

H: Have one sentence about the problem behavior ready. Stick to the facts, and avoid words that convey judgment. For example, "Yesterday you posted a comment on my page about my hair."

(Notice the phrase is "posted a comment," not "posted a *rude* comment." *Rude* is an emotionally charged word that's likely to make your friend defensive. Stick with the facts at first; feelings will come next.)

E: Express yourself. "I feel really embarrassed when you make comments like that about me, online or in person."

A: Ask for what you want or need. "I would really appreciate it if you didn't write or say things that you know make me feel insecure, like telling embarrassing stories or making fun of my hair."

R: Reiterate what you want, and explain how it will help both of you. "I want to feel like we can joke around without playing on each other's insecurities. Do you think we can work on this?"

(Notice the suggestion is "we," not "you." That word choice indicates that you're open to working on things too if she brings them up.)

D: Don't get sidetracked. If she gets defensive, stick to the point, or the goal at hand. "We can talk about other situations in a minute, but right now we're talking about this issue. Let's resolve it first. Can you try to stop? Do you need me to do anything to remind you?"

Another way to approach a difficult conversation is to use the "sandwich" technique. Think of the assertive statement as the sticky part (the peanut butter), sandwiched between two positive statements (the bread) that will encourage her to listen and engage in the conversation. Here's an example:

Bread: "Sarah, you are one of my closest friends."

Peanut butter: "I feel really embarrassed when you tease me. Can you please stop?"

Bread: "Thanks for being a good friend and listening."

Even if she isn't acting as a good friend, this is a good way to end it. She once was a good friend, and you want her to remember that.

What to Do When...

If you've seen lots of movies, you're familiar with the idea of the plot twist. That's when something unexpected happens, causing a complication in the story. Plot twists happen all the time in everyday life as well. Here's one: What if she doesn't stop the teasing or starts doing it even more?

If your friend has started to act more like a frenemy, she may be showing her true colors, which are not pretty. It's like someone coming on the set of your movie and talking trash about it—on purpose. As the director of this project, you don't stoop to her level; you use your directing skills instead. "I would really appreciate it if you would stop. This isn't funny to me anymore."

Remember the R in HEARD: reiterate your intentions and what you want from her. And keep your emotions in check. Like a little kid trying to get on your nerves, a frenemy will thrive when she knows she's hit an emotional trigger point. So try to hold it together, tears and all, until she's out of your sight. You may need to physically leave the situation to gather your thoughts and get clear. "All right, I told you how I felt, and I'd like it if you would please stop. I'm going to get out of here for a while. Let's talk when we've both had a chance to chill out."

Don't let this person make you feel that you are wrong. You spoke your mind, and if she's unwilling to act like a friend, you may have to reevaluate why you are friends with her in the first place.

Reflection Questions: Have you ever been taunted or teased to the point that it hurt your feelings? How did you handle it? If that situation were to occur again in the future, what would you say or do?

Write Your Script: Now it's your turn. Think of a friend who may be taking the "just kidding" comments a little too far. Write your script for talking to her.

Been There, Done That—Advice from Women and Girls Who've Been in Your Shoes

Ruby Karp is a fourteen-year-old comedian, journalist, feminist, and blogger for Hello Giggles and Mashable. She is currently heading to high school, and in her free time, she hosts a comedy show in New York City. Ruby knows a thing or two about being brave and speaking up, but she's also no stranger to typical teenage problems like dealing with mean girls.

Getting away from a frenemy is tricky. I've had one, and it's hard. I knew I'd have to see her every day at school, we have mutual friends, and if I were to tell her that I wanted to end the friendship, she would

make my life a total nightmare. My advice to you is to do what I did—slowly fade away from her. I started to hang out with different friend groups at school, sat at other lunch tables, and met up with other friends after school. I even made new friends. You can't just tell someone that you don't want to be friends anymore and all the reasons why you think they are a terrible friend because that's just mean and adds more drama to your life, but your actions can speak louder than words. You'll find new people, good people, to spend your time with, and they will help you get through it. It can be scary, but trust me it's so much better than being friends with a mean girl.

Ready to move on to another situation? This one's just as common, and just as likely to end a friendship if you don't deal with it effectively.

Director's Note

Show respect in the face of disrespect.

#ExpressYourself

The Situation: Saying No to Moochers

I got my driver's license before most of my friends. I feel like a chauffeur sometimes, especially with this one friend. She gives me an attitude if I can't drive her home or if I don't want to take her wherever she wants to go. She never offers to pay for gas even though I take her home from school most days. I feel guilty when I can't help her out and guilty when I give in to her demands. How do I deal with the guilt?

You may be the sweetest, kindest girl in the room, but that doesn't keep you safe from hurt feelings, frustrations, or frenemies. If you have a hard time saying no, people will push you around until you give in, and then you end up feeling disrespected. Whether your friend asks to borrow a few bucks for lunch, join your Saturday plans without an invite, or bum a ride after school, it can be difficult to say no, even when doing so is in your best interest. If going to grab a burger with your buds is going to make you late for your curfew or filling up your tank is taking away from your savings account, you are losing this game. It's like watching a rerun of your favorite TV show: you know what's going to happen and how you're going to feel, but you're powerless to change the outcome.

The scene needs a rewrite, and the goal is to maintain your self-respect. Speaking up may be uncomfortable, but if you don't, you won't get the respect you deserve.

Before You Say a Word

In this situation, as always, you need to identify your feelings. But you also need to take an objective look at the situation—in other words, get real and ask yourself what's reasonable. How would you treat a friend in your position? Be fair and give her the benefit of the doubt. Maybe she thinks you're happy to give her rides all the time. Both can be true—that she's not intending to disrespect you *and* that you feel disrespected. At the same time, it's true that you deserve to decide when it works for you and when it doesn't.

While you're being fair, ask yourself what you're doing to perpetuate the situation. Is it partly your fault? If so, own it.

And don't forget to identify your goals. Your general goals may be to maintain your self-respect and to get your friend to change her inconsiderate behavior. More specifically, the goal might be to have her share the cost of gas or compensate you in some other way for driving. Or maybe you just don't want to drive her around all the time, which is totally understandable. Even if she's good company (hey, she's got great playlists!), you may not want to be her chauffeur. So your goal might be to cut down on the driving time without kicking her to the curb altogether.

Set the Scene

Ideally, you should speak up before buckling up. There is no perfect location for the conversation. Just bring it up the next time she asks for a ride.

What to Say

Speaking up to get your needs met doesn't have to be a battle. You can do this super casually, with a gentle, friendly tone. (Remember, even if you're wiggling in your shoes just thinking about it, you can *act* casual and *act* from a place of self-respect.) Here's an outline of the script:

* brief comment about the topic

* how it affects you

* your request

* how what you're asking for will help both of you

Start with a casual opener. "Hey, my gas guzzler is running on empty these days."

Consider including some of your feelings to gain empathy. "I'm feeling super stressed about money. I'm happy to give you a ride, but could you pitch in for gas?"

Then add in how it will make you feel better. "Gas is expensive; I'd appreciate the help."

Here's a tip that applies to similar situations where you feel taken advantage of: don't apologize for asking for what you deserve. It makes you appear insecure. A director apologizes for things she's done wrong, but not what she deserves.

What to Do When...

Of course you hope that your friend will be understanding and agreeable. But here comes the plot twist: What if she says no or gets mad at you for asking?

When your request is met with a challenge, you can do a few things and still maintain your self-respect: stick to the request, negotiate, or accept that you are at a crossroads. It won't hurt to listen and try to understand your friend's point of view. You may totally disagree, and that's okay, but giving her a chance to express how she sees things will give you a window into her thought process. When you are able to see her side, you don't necessarily have to agree or give in, but it could help you understand where she's coming from. The more information you have about the other person's view, the better—you're not assuming; she's telling you what's on her mind. You can compromise or stretch your boundaries too, but hopefully not to the point of offering something you'll later regret. Try restating what you said about the problem and reiterating how it affects you. Then add a cooperative question, such as "How can we make this work for both of us?" or "What suggestions do you have?" The more information you can gather from this first conversation about fairness, the more prepared you'll be for the next. Consider coming back to it after you've rewritten your script.

Reflection Questions: Have you ever been in a situation in which a friend was taking advantage of you? How did you handle it? Were you able to find a solution and maintain your self-respect?

Is there a friend in your life right now who tends to push up against your boundaries? What do you plan to do the next time that happens?

Write Your Script: Now it's your turn. What would you say to a moocher in your life? Write a script for this situation and refer back to the example if needed.

This last example is of a situation that goes beyond annoyance or hurt feelings and invites you to think about how you can be a true friend. When you're worried about a friend, it can be especially difficult to know what to say.

The Situation: Risky Behavior

My friend Margo has been wearing big bracelets on her arms, and recently I noticed she had some scars that weren't there last week. I asked her about the scars, and she told me she used to cut herself in middle school, but that was years ago. I'm really worried she'll wind up in the hospital, or worse. What do I do?

Teenagers have a lot to deal with and sometimes handle stress in ineffective or dangerous ways. Having difficulty managing anxiety, depression, or any difficult emotion can lead to harmful behaviors—eating disorders, drug and alcohol abuse, self-injury, or even suicide. As a friend of someone who's harming herself, you're likely to be conflicted about whether to keep her secret or to try to get her some professional help. You can be her best bud, but you can't be her therapist or doctor.

Before You Say a Word

One way to help your friend is by helping her face her problem and get treatment. Many people who get professional help do so because a friend gave them the support and encouragement they needed during trying times. Before talking to your friend, give some serious thought on how to approach the subject. If you don't want to bring it up yourself, share the information with a parent, a counselor, or another trusted adult who can help you figure out how to help her. Remember this can be hard for you too, so reach out to someone who can help make you feel more confident before starting the conversation with your friend. Check out the list of resources at the back of this book, too.

Set the Scene

Be aware of your environment, and be discreet. Respect your friend's privacy, and don't talk to other friends about it.

Sometimes people gossip or spread rumors when they don't know what else to do. Think about what you would want your friend to do if you were in her shoes. Then find a time that's safe and comfortable to talk to her. Avoid crowded areas and places where you're likely to be interrupted. A quiet place might be best, either at school—so you can accompany her to talk to a favorite teacher or counselor—or at home, so the two of you can talk to a parent.

What to Say

Like the sandwich technique presented earlier, the following formula will help you package what you want to say in a kind and caring way. Try organizing it like this:

* caring comment

* expression of concern

* possible solutions

* positive comment about your friendship

Here's an example: "Margo, you are one of my best friends. I don't want to upset you, and I need to tell you that I'm seriously worried about those scars on your arm. It makes me nervous to know that you could really hurt yourself. So I want to help you. I know if I were cutting or something like that, you would want to help me too. Can we go talk to the counselor or your mom? I really want to help, I want us to be friends forever, and I want you to be happy."

Notice that the second sentence has the word "and" instead of "but." The word "but" is a trigger word, and you may want to avoid it. Most people hear it and automatically become defensive or emotionally charged. The word "and" has a more positive association. The listener will remain listening, instead of thinking *Oh no, what is she about to say?* or acting defensive. Expressing serious concern is a good way to get your friend to listen. Being assertive and offering a few choices is the best way to encourage her to get help.

What to Do When...

It can be hard, of course, to predict your friend's response. What if she gets mad at you? Or makes you promise not to tell? Or threatens you, saying she'll tell your secrets or end your friendship?

If your friend is doing something that is seriously harmful or concerning, it is likely that the behavior is a way of coping—it's something she feels she needs. She might act angry or emotional because she sees you as trying to take that away from her. That's the risk you take when you attempt to help a friend. Think about it this way: if her behavior were to get worse—whether it be cutting, disordered eating, drug abuse, or some other kind of self-harm—and you didn't say or do anything, how would you feel?

If she's resisting your help, the next step is to tell her you're going to talk to a trusted adult. Be strong and remind yourself you are doing this to help her get the support she needs. It's about something bigger than keeping a secret; it may be about saving her life. If she says no or gets mad, realize that she's acting from a fearful mindset. Her unhealthy coping skill is being revealed, and that's uncomfortable. Let her know that you love her and you're not comfortable keeping it to yourself because it's about her safety.

Here's an example: "Margo, I understand that this is making you mad, and I'm sorry. But it's too big of a secret for me to keep, and I know I need to help you stay safe. I can tell your parents, my parents, or the counselor—you choose."

Giving her a choice about who you tell is a way of giving her some power. If she's willing to make the choice, great. If not, go right to the counselor and ask for an appointment that day. (If you feel that your friend's life is in danger, of course you should let the staff know that it's an emergency.) They are professionals, and they know how to handle these kinds of situations effectively while avoiding embarrassment. Your friend may be temporarily angry, but it's likely that she'll be grateful later on. It may even make your friendship stonger.

One last thing to consider: This is a tough situation for anyone. It could be helpful for you to talk to a counselor or other trusted adult who can help you deal with the intense emotions that may come up. Be sure to take care of yourself.

Reflection Questions: Have you ever felt concerned about a friend's safety? Do you have a friend right now who you think might be hurting herself? What do you think it would feel like to hold on to a big secret like that?

Have you ever told a friend a secret in the hopes that she would help you get support?

Write Your Script: Now it's your turn. Think of a friend whose behavior was worrying you, and write your script.

The situations presented in this chapter are common struggles for girls of all ages—and adults too! You'll find that the skills and scripts that relate to each scenario can also apply to many other friendship dilemmas.

The next chapter will present strategies for talking to the people who play the role of "producers" in your life—your parents and other family members. Even when they aren't on the set, they often make decisions that affect how you direct your movie. Learning to approach family conflicts with assertiveness will not only improve your home life; it will give you a chance to practice skills that will make the rest of your relationships easier as well.

True friends are hard to find. So when you find someone worthy of your friendship, hang on tight.

Director's Note

Chose to spend your time with those who lift
you up, not weigh you down.

#ExpressYourself

Chapter 3

Family Frustrations & Building Better Bonds

Your true tribe will always want you to be happy above all else;
they're just scared for you. Make sure you're happy with your
decision and radiate that, and others will cheer you on.

— Alexis Wolfer, Founder, TheBeautyBean.com

As you embark on your new role as "director" of your life, your parents are in the role of the "producers." They often have a big say in the decisions you make—even if you wish they didn't. Producers give the green light (the "okay") in the movie-making process. They decide how the money is spent and where the director can shoot, and they might even have some control over the script. If they feel that the content is inappropriate, you'll have to convince them otherwise or it won't be part of the movie.

An assertive style can help you get what you want or need from your family. It shows your family members that you are growing and maturing and that you deserve to be treated like the young adult you are becoming. Acting assertively shows that you respect yourself and the other people in your life—in this case, your family members.

This doesn't mean you have to agree with them—far from it. It means that you express yourself in such a way that you respect both their views and your own. Your assertiveness shapes how others respond to you, and it helps train them how to treat you. Your mom may expect you to whine when she says no, for example. But if instead, you put your new skills into practice, she may see that you've got it together. Over time, she'll give you more freedom, opportunities, and respect.

Your Rights

In your family, roles are important. Mom or Dad may have the final say for good reason, but you still have certain rights and privileges.

* You have the right to give your opinion.

* You have the right to share your feelings.

* You have the right to ask for what you want or need.

* You have the right to respectfully disagree.

* You have the right to offer your ideas and suggestions.

This chapter will show you how these rights apply in different situations and help you figure out how to assert them.

Making Adjustments

As you grow into a more independent person, your parents may have a hard time letting go of your younger self. As a kid, you didn't always get to make your own choices; your parents made decisions about everything from your bedtime to your homework habits. When you were little, you needed that kind of caretaking; you needed guidance. Eventually, though, kids grow up and become teenagers; and as a teen, it's your job to develop more autonomy and to create your own identity, separate from your parents'. It's not only normal but necessary for you to come up with your own thoughts, opinions, and values; it's what prepares you for adulthood.

Parents often have trouble adjusting to this change. It takes time to get used to "the new you." It can be scary for them, as they realize that you're closer to leaving home and heading off to college or living on your own.

It's not just your parents who might have trouble with this. Your siblings and extended family can also forget (or choose not to recognize) that you're becoming an adult. Your desire to go on a date or to a party may freak out your grandparents and your parents. Meanwhile, your siblings may be jealous or confused about your newfound fashion sense. Everyone in your life has to do a little adjusting. Problems arise when you forget that they're struggling with your transition to adulthood. It can be hurtful when the people close to you don't seem to value the person you're becoming. However, it's not just about you, and acknowledging this truth can help you prevent future conflicts and misunderstandings. This chapter will give you the skills you need to be authentic, and at the same time empathic so you can keep these relationships strong. It will be a lot easier to show your family how to treat you when you can see things from their perspective.

What You Need to Know About Your Parents

Here are some things to keep in mind:

* Your parents are scared. They aren't trying to ruin your life—though it may feel like it. They're probably afraid that you'll become like the teens they see on reality TV or on the news. Unfortunately their fear can sometimes run the show. (Remember that while you can't change *people*, with a few strategies you can change their *behavior*. Your parents' behavior is not magically going to change unless you show them with your actions and your words how you want to be treated.)

* You reflect them. Parents may, at times, put too much emphasis on this, but it's true—the decisions you make are a reflection of your family. The things you post online, the clothes you wear, and the way you treat others reflect you and your family. All these things may lead to pride, embarrassment, or even disappointment.

* They want you to be happy, not miserable. Parents want to protect you from making potentially dangerous decisions. Sometimes they forget to express this; or they try to, but it comes out as controlling or unfair—which sucks. Remember, they're new to this teen thing, too.

* They don't *have* to do all the things they do for you. They *choose* to. Yes, they're responsible for keeping

you safe, fed, and cared for. That doesn't mean they have to pay for a new phone, dance classes, or the new jeans you've been eyeing. There is no law that says they must, so when they do things like that, they do it because they want you to be happy and comfortable. Most parents look for opportunities to make their kids' lives easier and better. What they want is for you to appreciate what they give you, rather than taking it for granted.

Actions Speak Louder than Words

It's easy for feelings to get hurt when you and your parents have different opinions. Complicated issues—like the types of friends you hang out with and your attitude about sex and drugs—can cause arguments for all sorts of reasons. This sucks, but you've still got to interact with your family everyday.

Your parents, of course, have the power advantage. Not only because they make the rules, but because they have a lot more experience with arguing, negotiating, and expressing themselves. Teens haven't had a lot of practice with these skills, and parents sometimes forget that. (It's ironic, right? They expect you to communicate like an adult, even when they treat you like a kid!)

You can help the situation by doing your best not to act like a child, because acting like one will surely result in being treated like one. Throwing a fit, storming off, slamming the door, or making threats will show your parents that you aren't mature; nor are you ready for more freedom. If you can't control yourself, why would they let you go to that party or give you the keys to the car? And if you want your parents to understand you, trust you, and respect you, communication is key. Ignoring them or giving one-word responses like "Fine" does nothing to bridge the gap and is unlikely to get you what you want.

Admit it: as much as you want to run your own life, you need their help. When you speak and act assertively, your parents will start to take you seriously. It may take a little time, but you can speed things along by increasing all kinds of positive communication. Notice the little things they do for you and thank them. When your dad remembers your favorite cereal or your mom lends you her earrings, let them know you appreciate it; doing so goes a long way. Later, when you ask for something else, they'll be more likely to say yes.

Director's Note

When you speak and act assertively,
everyone will take you seriously.

#ExpressYourself

Getting Parents to Say Yes

If you have a history of fighting with your parents, they will surely take notice when you decide to take a different approach. If, however, you ask for something that same day, they may see it as manipulation, rather than a genuine step toward maturity. So instead, try to add this new approach into your everyday life. Make it a habit. The main thing you will need to show them is that you're responsible. When they can see it, they will believe it. (A couple of ways to do this are keeping your room clean, doing your chores without reminders, cleaning up the kitchen after your parents have prepared a meal, and setting the table while they're cooking. Here's the key: do these things *before* being asked. Shock them in a good way!)

Say you want a car, a new computer, or maybe you want to take a fun trip with your friends. Prior to saying yes or no, parents think about how responsible you've been recently: *Can she take care of a car, keep it clean, and remember to fill it up with gas?* Figure out small ways to show them you are responsible.

If you show that you want to contribute to the family and that you don't resent your responsibilities, you will be seen in a whole different light—a more grown-up light. When that happens, you'll have a much higher success rate when you ask for what you want.

Including Your Parents in Your Life

If the only time you speak to your parents is when you need something, they'll be conditioned to think that is your intention every time you start a conversation. Similarly, if most of your conversations with your parents are arguments, they'll be defensive before you even say a word. One way to break this pattern is to talk to them more often about the little things in your daily life. Tell them about your friends ("My friend Maya got the lead in the school play"). Give them a sense of who these people are. Then, when you ask to sleep over at a friend's house, they might be less hesitant than they would be if they had never heard her name.

Here's another idea: instead of waiting for your parents to bombard you with that question you hate—"How's school?"—consider starting up the conversation instead. Mention a book you're reading for English class or something interesting you recently learned about in school. If you're exhausted and not in the mood to chitchat, tell them: "Can we talk at dinner? I'm tired right now."

Advantages of Empathy

Your parents have never been in your shoes. When they were your age, things were different. But keep in mind that you have never been in their shoes either. You don't experience running a household, parenting, paying bills, and dealing with all sorts of other adult issues. This is why empathy is such an important part of being assertive. When you try to place yourself in your parents' shoes, you will automatically do a better job of communicating in an empathic and effective way. And you will be heard.

It can be challenging, of course, to be considerate toward your parents when you feel like they're always on your case about something. But get this: empathy breeds more empathy—in other words, you're showing them how to treat you. The more they feel like you understand—or are trying to understand—them, the more they're likely to understand you, and perhaps give you what you're looking for. Even a simple "How was your day?" can have a huge impact because it shows that you *see* them, and that you understand that the whole world doesn't revolve around you.

Here's an example of empathy in action: Your mom looks upset after getting off the phone with her sister. You don't have to play the part of her therapist, but a simple, "Anything I can do to help?"—or just a hug or a smile—will show that you care about her and not just about yourself. (It also totally helps bust the stereotype that teens only think about themselves!) These kinds of actions add up. They show your parents you are becoming more mature.

Again, don't just do this immediately before you ask a favor. Parents will see through that and view it as fake. Make it a habit so they know that this is the new you! Start building up your "empathy bank" now, and you'll see that your parents will respond more positively when you want something from them in the future.

Your Own Unique Family

This chapter will present some specific scenarios that you may encounter with your parents and siblings and give you ideas for how to handle them assertively and effectively. To get you started, here's an exercise that will get you thinking about your family in particular, what works with them, and what you might want to do differently.

Exercise: Assess Your Audience

Assertiveness is something we put into practice spontaneously, but as you're learning and practicing the skills presented in this book, it will help to do everything you can to prepare for moments of opportunity. This exercise is intended to help you take a deeper look at how you and your family interact so figuring out how to get your needs met won't be such a guessing game.

Acting assertively isn't magic; it's more like science. That means you'll have to do a little research—in this case, on your family. Behaviors can tell you a lot more than words. When you take a step back and observe how others behave, it can make a huge difference in how you choose to communicate.

For instance, if you've noticed that your mom is usually in a good mood when she gets off the phone with one of her friends, you might conclude that would be a good time to ask her for some extra cash. How are these two things related? Well, if your mom's like most people, she'll likely be more generous and easygoing if she's already in a good mood. On the contrary, if she's usually in a bad mood when she gets home from work, asking her for something at that time would not put the odds in your favor. Knowing when the time is right is an important part of being an effective communicator.

If we were in science class, we would call this *behaviorism*—increasing the behaviors you want (her shelling out cash) by waiting until the right moment to ask. If you can't control the timing—say you're on your way out with friends and need some money—you can use other behavioral clues to figure out how to make your request in the most effective way possible. (More on this later in the chapter.)

Awareness of others is essential if you're trying to avoid arguments and get what you want. The first question to ask yourself is: Who's your audience? If you go into a meeting, for example, without doing any research on the people you're trying to impress, you're not likely to make a good impression. So think of your parents as the producers of your show, and consider what would make them likely to buy into your project. The way to do this is to focus on what you already know about them. Give some thought to the following questions and then answer them, either in your mind or in your journal. Try to be honest with yourself—this is just research, like the research you would do for a big paper for school. But instead of finding the information with Google or asking your friends what they'd do, you'll get the answer by taking a look at your own experience with your family.

- When was the last time you got your parents to say yes to something? Where were you? What were they doing when you asked them? What kind of mood were they in before you asked? Did you have to convince them, or did they say yes right away?

- Can you remember a time when your parents said no to some-thing, and then you convinced them to change their mind? Maybe it was buying you a game system, letting you get your ears pierced, or agreeing to a later curfew. How did you get them to give in?

- Are there certain times when your parents are particularly stressed or in a bad mood? Identify the situations or times of day that are not ideal for asking for something from your parents.

- What are some of the things your parents want you to do more of? Chores? Homework? Being nice to your sister or brother? What expectations do they have of you as a member of the family?

- Are there ways you've reacted in the past (yelling, crying, name-calling, threatening, door-slamming) that were obviously unhelpful in getting you what you wanted? If so, what did your parents do to trigger that response in you?

- Are there times when you get along especially well with your siblings? When? What is it about those situations that make things go more smoothly?

Look over your answers and notice the times when your family responded to you in a positive way. What influenced their decision to give you what you wanted? Was it the time of day? Your chill attitude? Were they rewarding you for a history of positive behaviors?

It's important to identify how your own behavior shapes their responses and to remember that if you want a different outcome, you may have to do things differently. If, for example, your parents are hesitating to let you have friends over because you often leave a mess in the kitchen, you'll probably need to do a better job cleaning up. If it's not totally clear what you need to do differently, just try making some changes. Their behavior in response to these changes will tell you whether you're on the right track.

Director's Note

Treat others the way you want to be treated.
Kind actions are confident ones.

#ExpressYourself

Putting Your Skills to Work

The situations presented in this chapter are ones that are frequently experienced by teenagers. If a scenario doesn't seem to apply to you right now, see if the skills and scripts could fit another situation you're struggling with—most of these techniques can be used with anyone. Share them with a friend who may be having a hard time with his or her parents; or just keep in mind that the situations could come up for you, and being prepared is key in staying confident. It's worth asking yourself, What would I do if I were in this situation? or How would I help guide someone else through this? Having some ideas about how to handle different situations will increase your confidence—and your chances of success—in the future.

The Situation: My Parents Won't Let Me Grow Up

My parents are so overprotective. My mom checks my phone and e-mail, and even tracks my phone to see where I am after school. She always knows where I am and what I'm doing. I have never done anything—online or off-line—that would give her a reason not to trust me. I really want to get a new app on my phone that all my friends have—one that lets us chat and stuff. I am the only one that doesn't have it and am missing out on all the conversations. She thinks it's bad and says no way. How can I convince her that I'm mature enough to decide these things for myself?

You are not alone. Many parents are afraid of what they see on the news, what they hear your friends are doing, or what they imagine could happen to you. Keep in mind that your mom's intention isn't to keep you from enjoying life, but to keep you safe. In situations like this, no doesn't always mean no if you know how to assert yourself and negotiate.

Before You Say a Word

Start preparing for your conversation with your mother by identifying your goal. If the goal is to get what you want, remember that it almost never works to ask for everything you want all at once. When it comes to negotiation, prioritizing is important. Choose one thing for starters, and then use that to work toward earning more trust, which will lead to more freedom in the long run. In this case, it sounds as if you'll want to start by talking about the app.

Before your talk, do some brainstorming. Think of all the possible reasons she wouldn't want you to have the app. Is she worried about whom you're hanging out with? Afraid you'll post or receive something inappropriate? Think about how you can empathize with her, how you can let her know you recognize where her hesitation is coming from. This doesn't mean you agree; it just means you can see why she feels the way she does.

Set the Scene

Give some thought to the right time and place to have this conversation. Talking in the car, at an event, or while she's doing something that requires her attention may not be in your best interest. A quiet environment with few distractions almost always works best. You might also want to have access to your phone or computer in case you want to show her how the app works. Be sure to set aside enough time so you don't end up rushing through the conversation. It takes time to listen to another person's views, to express your own, and to respond to each other thoughtfully.

What to Say

Here's a technique that will help you stay on track. It's called *ASK*—it stands for Asking, Showing, and Knowing.

A: Ask your mom if she has time to explore the issue with you. Let her know that you want to look at the app with her and explain how you and your friends will use it.

S: Show her the app or the website, as well as reviews from parents or other information that that might address her concerns. If you've done your research, you might even be able to show her websites with information and advice about how to keep kids safe.

K: Communicate that you know and understand her concerns. You could say, for example, "We both know that there are risks that go along with getting this app. I don't want to receive inappropriate messages or get in trouble." Then, to address her concerns, let her have the password, or show her how you're using it. Ask if she's open to compromise and come up with a suggestion. Let her know that your intent is to show her that you can be trusted.

What to Do When...

What if she still says no? Well, it may not be her final answer if she hasn't heard everything yet. A skillful negotiator keeps a few strategies in her back pocket, just in case. Remember, if the goal is getting what you want, you may have to pace yourself. Give it a few hours or days, and then come back with another idea or another possible plan. Or ask more questions. (You can't read her mind, so you might need to ask what she's thinking.) Collect more evidence that proves your point, and give her more time to consider it. Take that time to show her how responsible you are in other areas of your life.

Practice purposeful persistence: Ask what you can do to earn her trust. Figure out the reason she's still saying no, and then ask what you need to do to make it a yes. If you get an unhelpful response, dig further: "Okay, you want me to be more mature. I want that too. How can I show you that I am?" Be careful not to bombard her with questions, and try not to lose your cool. Those are easy ways to blow it. "It's not fair" or "everyone else gets to" will also get you in a deeper hole. Remember, you're trying to act like the adult you're becoming, not the toddler who threw tantrums to get her way.

This kind of negotiation is all about balancing your needs with the needs of your parents—respecting them while respecting yourself. Finding a balance like this can be hard, but it will be worth it in the long run.

Reflection Questions: Are there things you wish your parents would be less overprotective about? What are they? Why do you think your parents are so overprotective? What are they worried will happen? What could you do to put their mind more at ease?

As a little girl, how did you show them you deserved a little more responsibility? Maybe it was getting them to give you a later bedtime, dropping you off at the mall alone, or picking out your back-to-school clothes. What did you say or do to prove that you were ready for the responsibility?

Been There, Done That—Advice from Women Who've Been in Your Shoes

Alexis Jones is the founder of I Am That Girl, an author, an internationally recognized speaker, a media personality, and an activist.

During college I wanted to study abroad in Spain. It was a lifelong dream of mine, but my parents were not supportive. Our parents' job is to protect us, but sometimes they want to protect us so much that they protect us from really living. We have to teach people how to treat us and negotiate and renegotiate our boundaries, especially with the ones we love the most. I reminded my mom that she didn't raise me to let no get in the way of authoring my own life and following my dreams: "I can understand that you've spent the past twenty years of my life doing everything in your power to protect me. I can imagine how scary it would be, the thought of me on my own, halfway across the world where you can't protect me from every possible danger. I don't expect you to understand every life decision I make, but I do hope you can be supportive of the things that are important to me, and this is one of them. I love you, and I would never be reckless with my life or jeopardize the lifetime you've spent protecting me." I spent that summer in Seville with the support of my parents and came home safe and sound. You have to fight for the things that are important to you. That discussion with my mom was the first time I stood my ground, and she respected me for it. Be bold. Be brave. Chase your passion and stop at nothing.

The Situation: I'm Living in a "War Zone"

My parents argue all the time. When they were married, the only way they communicated was by yelling. Now that they are divorced, they can't even be in the same room together. What's even worse is that whenever I'm spending "quality time" with one of them, that parent is constantly complaining about the other one. It's like being in the middle of a war zone. I'd rather stay in my room than hang out with either one of them. I don't want to tell them how I feel because I'm afraid they'll get mad at me. What do I do?

Who wouldn't be nervous about speaking up in this situation, especially when your parents have shown you that they don't communicate their emotions well? The challenge here is to find a way to express yourself honestly while maintaining your relationship with your parents and without starting another fight. It sounds tricky, but it may be easier than you think!

Before You Say a Word

In chapter 1, we discussed the three goals of assertive communication. One of those is building or maintaining a relationship. Before deciding to hibernate in your room for good, give the sandwich technique a try. You're going to put your sandwich together with the basic peanut butter and bread, but you're going to add a little jelly (some sweet stuff) to help get your audience to listen.

Set the Scene

Think of your preparation for your talk as packing a lunch. You're not going to eat it first thing in the morning; you're making it for later. As always, you'll want to find the right time to approach your parents (individually in this case)—maybe on a walk, or after dinner, when no one's in a rush. One-on-one is usually best. Having siblings or friends around could lead to embarrassment or defensiveness on their end.

What to Say

The "bread" in your sandwich is how you frame your request: "Hey, Dad, I have something I want to talk to you about. Do you have a sec?"

The "peanut butter" is the content—what you want to communicate: "It's upsetting when I hear you and Mom arguing. I feel caught in the middle and that bothers me. I'd feel a lot better if you could try not to argue in front of me." In order to be spreadable, the peanut butter should be smooth. That means your approach needs to be kind and gentle.

The jelly is how you "sweeten up" what you're saying so that it's easier to swallow. Empathy always works well: "It must be really hard to be in your position," or "I know that Mom can be difficult to talk to." You can spread the jelly before the peanut butter if you think it will work better that way.

Then close your "sandwich" with another piece of bread: "It would make me feel a lot better if you could work on this. I'll talk to Mom too and ask her to do the same."

What to Do When...

What if the conversation gets too hot to handle? If emotions are running high, it can be hard to stay focused on what you want to say. Consider writing it out. A letter or e-mail can be a great way to make sure you're following your script and communicating assertively. Plus, it will allow your parent time in private to think about how he's behaving and how it's affecting you. You can use the sandwich technique for your letter as well.

Reflection Questions: Have you ever been in a situation like this? Maybe your parents don't argue with you but with others when you're around—how do you handle it? Do they listen?

If such a situation were to occur again in the future, what would you say or do?

Write Your Script: Now it's your turn. It's likely you've been put in the middle of two friends, parents, or family members. Write the script to get the outcome you desire.

The Situation: My Sibling Is So Disrespectful

I have a problem with my sister. She always takes my things without asking—my clothes, my makeup, my cell phone charger, everything. She doesn't respect my privacy at all. She just comes into my room and takes my stuff. It's infuriating! How do I get her to stop?

Siblings are notorious for disrespecting each other, especially by taking or using each other's things without asking. When your sister does this, it might feel like she's doing it just to push your buttons. Whatever the reason, there is a simple solution to getting her to understand how you feel and to change her behavior. The key is to take an assertive but casual approach—not an aggressive or argumentative one, which is sure to spark defensiveness. Stick to the simple script in this chapter. You may have to have this conversation multiple times, but over time it will likely stop her disrespectful behavior.

Before You Say a Word

Remember that your goal is to get your sister to stop taking your stuff, not to start a fight. Make sure you're calm before confronting your sister. She'll be able to hear any annoyance or frustration in your voice, so even if that's how you're feeling, do your best to act casual. Don't go into the conversation making assumptions about things you're not sure about. It's always better to ask—and give her the benefit of the doubt—than to assume. Also, be ready to acknowledge if the behavior goes both ways. If you took her shirt last week without asking, admit it.

Set the Scene

It's easy to succumb to the urge to text your sister when you have something to say—but don't give in to it. For this kind of conversation, the most effective way to communicate is in person. Tone gets lost in texts and instant messages; it's easier to understand how someone feels when you can see her face. Don't put yourself through the anxiety of waiting for her to respond (or not) to your text.

What to Say

You may have to rehearse this script out loud to make sure you can say it without sounding angry, sarcastic, or fake. Remember, the goal is to sound relaxed.

In a casual tone: "Hey, have you seen my pink sweater?"

Or if you know she has it: "Hey, can I please have my pink sweater back?"

If you have something to own up to: "I know sometimes I take your things without asking too. I will do my best to stop doing that. I know it can be really frustrating for both of us when we take each other's stuff without asking first."

Ask for what you want: "Can you ask me before borrowing something next time?"

Don't overexplain, as in telling her why you need it or pointing out that it ruined your day because you didn't have it. A simple request will do the trick. Most importantly, do *not* give in to the urge to go into her room and grab it without saying anything. Invading her space will just make her feel justified in continuing to invade yours. Instead, model the respectful behavior you'd like to see from her. Asking is key. If you want her to communicate with you, you need to be willing to do the same.

If you need another strategy, you can always try the sandwich approach, explained earlier in this chapter. Maybe a little empathy will help: "I'm sure you didn't mean to be disrespectful; you were probably just in a rush or something. But I just get so irritated when I can't find my things."

What to Do When...

What if she gets defensive? It's frustrating when that happens, but you can take it as a signal to get back on track and reiterate your purpose: "I really want to work on a solution so we don't have to have this conversation anymore. How about both of us ask before we enter each other's room? What do you think?" Asking for her opinion makes the conversation feel more cooperative, like you're both on the same side. You can even say something about how making this agreement will help your relationship—you both will feel less stressed and less angry at each other.

If her reaction is really unreasonable or dramatic, try to stay cool instead of getting pulled into an argument. Tell her you can talk about it another time. You may feel like she didn't hear you, but she must have—otherwise she wouldn't be so upset. Let her sit with it for a bit, and when she's in a calmer state of mind, try again.

Reflection Questions: Do you and your sibling(s) get along? Do you find that you get into the same fights all the time? What are they about?

How can you handle yourself in an assertive way next time an argument arises? What will you say or do differently?

Write Your Script: Now it's your turn. Write a script for getting someone to stop pushing your buttons and start respecting you. It doesn't have to be a sibling or family member.

The Situation: My Parents Just Don't Understand!

I failed my math midterm, and now my parents are grounding me until I get my grades up, which could take months! The problem is they think I'm not studying hard enough. They say I'm lazy and spend too much time texting. I've tried to explain that I don't understand my teacher, and all they said was, "You should have asked for help earlier." They don't get it—I'm doing the best I can! How can I get them to hear me and help me?

Sometimes parents assume they know what's best when they really don't. Or they jump to trying to solve the problem for you rather than listening to how you're feeling, which is so annoying. Remember, acting assertive shows your parents that you respect yourself, and that will lead to more respect from them as well.

Before You Say a Word

First, get clear about your goal. Is it to get them to change their tone with you? To get you some help with math? You can ask for both, but you might want to approach it one goal at a time. If your parents are already angry, they'll be less likely to hear you if they feel overwhelmed by your requests.

Check in with yourself too. Are you feeling upset or defensive? Are you *really* ready to sit down with them and listen to their suggestions? If you're feeling upset, try to calm down before speaking up. Otherwise, you're likely to get emotional, and they may end up focusing on that, rather than what you're asking for.

Set the Scene

Writing your script is often the hardest part. So here's where you might want to refer back to the HEARD acronym introduced in chapter 2. Here's a brief review of what it stands for:

* Have one sentence about the problem behavior ready.

* Express yourself.

* Ask for what you want or need.

* Reiterate what you want, and explain how it will help both of you.

* Don't get sidetracked.

What to Say

You're not asking for your privileges back yet. That will happen soon, but first you need your parents to see that you're suffering, that you share their concern, and that you want to do something about it—because when they can empathize with you, they will be better listeners and more likely to rethink their punishment. The HEARD acronym you just reviewed will help you cover all those bases.

* Have one sentence about the problem behavior. "I know I am doing poorly at school."

* Express yourself. "Please understand that I feel really bad about myself as it is."

* Ask for what you want or need. "I know you feel that it's important to punish me for my behavior, but can you help me fix the problem? I am nervous about school as it is, so grounding me just puts more pressure on me."

* Reiterate what you want, and explain how it will help both of you. "I don't expect you to just let me get off with no consequence, but can we talk about how to get what we all want—good grades?"

* Don't get sidetracked. Even if they up their anger or threats, try to keep calm and cool—you are showing that you are serious. A screaming match, slammed doors, or swearing at each other will only show them that you're immature, too much so to reason with.

Try not to be reactive. Responding with "That's not true! You don't get it!" will just tell them you're not mature enough to have such conversations. They won't see the adult you, who is trying so hard to assert herself. Instead, try validation and getting back to the point: "I know you think that I'm not trying. I feel like I am, but I'm confused by the material. Can we talk about how you can help me?"

What to Do When...

What if they stick to the punishment? This is where you practice your negotiation skills. That means switching from focusing on your feelings to focusing on the situation. Rather than expressing how you feel about their punishment or solution, come up with some of your own: "Instead of being grounded until my grades are better, can I earn back some of my privileges by going to tutorials twice a week until I'm caught up?" or "What if I turn in my phone while I'm doing my homework and then get it back when I'm finished?"

Ask your parents to think it over and get back to you. Think of it as a business deal—you want to be professional and keep it together until the papers are signed or the check is in your hand. Remember, they are the producers. If they still stick to their original plan, instead of acting immature, try your hardest to stay in an assertive and confident state of mind: "I'm disappointed by that" or "I hope we can try to talk about handling this some other way later." The less defensive and aggressive you get, the more mature you will look and the more respect you'll be given.

Reflection Questions: Have your parents ever been super unreasonable about something? How did you handle it? Did you get what you wanted?

How would you handle a disagreement with them in the future? What would you say to make sure they hear your point of view?

Write Your Script: Now it's your turn. Write your script using the HEARD technique to ask for something you want or need from a family member.

This chapter gave you a view into how to use your directing skills when you're in conflict with the "producers" of your show. But what about the "press"—the people who judge you, write about you, and promote your movie to the public? You connect with these people when you use social media, and they are not always people you know personally. The truth is, the things you post online and the people these posts connect you with all play a huge part in the way you're perceived by everyone in your life. The director often forgets that everything she says and does may end up public—whether she wants it that way or not. The next chapter will address communication in the digital world, and how to assert yourself when online drama unfolds.

Director's Note

Train others how to treat you by acting assertively.

#ExpressYourself

Chapter 4

Digital Drama & Texting Troubles

Sometimes, courage is just a whisper.

— Danielle LaPorte,
http://www.daniellelaporte.com/truthbomb

"Talking" to a friend can mean a lot of different things in the digital world. There are so many ways to communicate with others: texting, posting, messaging, chatting, snapping, Instagramming. As cool as it can be to talk without actually speaking, it can also be a big source of stress. Your digital footprint is made up of more than just the images you want the world to see—your profile picture, your posts, your likes, your pics, and your persona. It probably includes a lot of things you'd rather keep private. Unfortunately, these things can be all too easy to find online, and your digital footprint may last forever.

Technology provides a vast playground for exploring your interests, meeting and connecting with others, and figuring out who you are or who you want to be. While the teens of previous generations had to rely mostly on magazines and books for information and advice about fashion, dating, and friendship, you can view and create virtual pinboards, click through a blog, or ask Google for answers. There are endless options for exploring the world around you without even leaving your room.

Good Publicity vs. Bad Publicity

Have you ever heard the expression "There's no such thing as bad publicity"? That may be true for reality TV stars whose only goal is fame, but it's certainly not the case for most of us. If you care about other things in life—your relationships, your future career, your reputation—there's a big difference between good publicity and bad publicity. Your online image is important, and there are lots of ways to blow it.

As the director of your life, you have a lot of control over your own publicity. Celebrities who end up on the front page of the tabloids know the limits of their control—they've learned the hard way. They also know that the words and images that get circulated in the media can make or break their careers. So they hire experts—publicists, also known as public relations (PR) agents. Their job is to make sure their clients are represented in a positive light.

Publicists know how to navigate the complex world of online exposure. Their job becomes difficult, if not impossible, when the people they represent make impulsive decisions to text or tweet thoughtless comments or reveal too much personal information. When that happens, the publicist can try to put a "spin" on it, but those kinds of mistakes just can't be undone. Even "private" messages can easily be leaked. I'm sure you can think of a famous politician or movie star whose racy photos went viral and turned into headline news. Careers can be crushed by those heat-of-the-moment communications, and they remain forever on display, for the whole world to see.

We hear about these things when they happen to famous people. It's important to remember that they happen to not-so-famous people too—every day. If you don't want your reputation to take a hit (and you can't afford to hire a PR team), you have to act as your own PR agent. Being a responsible user of online media and controlling what you put out for others to see is essential if you want to avoid being a victim of bad publicity.

Expressing Yourself Online

What you like, post, text, tweet, and share online says a lot about you. The hundreds or thousands of people who see this information will make all sorts of judgments based on it. So respecting and asserting yourself are as important in the digital world as they are anywhere else in your life.

Online assertiveness isn't just about how you respond when someone writes "dislike" on your news feed, or about telling your mom to stop texting you while you're in class. It's about everything you do with your phone and computer. With every message and every photo, you're expressing who you are and how you want to be seen.

Think it doesn't matter if you complain about your teacher in a rant on your private page or post a picture you think your parents will never see? Think again. In fact, before posting anything, you should assume it will be seen by everyone—your teachers, your parents, your grandparents, your future boyfriend or girlfriend, the admissions department of the college you're applying to, your future employer. Remember that it never really goes away—even when you press delete, it's still stored somewhere. In other words, when it comes to digital communication, there's really no such thing as private.

Image Is Everything

If you think of the life you're creating every day as your movie, then your digital image is the trailer, or preview. Just as it only takes a few minutes to watch a preview and get the gist of a movie you're interested in, it takes a lot less time to do an online search than to meet someone in real life. So lots of people do this as the first step in connecting—or to see if they're interested. You wouldn't rent a movie without taking a look at the trailer or watching previews before making a decision would you? Teachers, colleges, new friends, friends' parents, staff at prospective jobs and internships—all these people (as well as people you haven't even thought of) will look at your profile and go by your digital reel to make a first impression or a final decision.

All these people are likely to scour your social media profiles to see your reputation before you even speak to them in real life. What this means is that even if you have a great GPA and the best manners on the planet, your online presence will factor in as well. Research shows that when college admissions staff look into students' online presence (Facebook, Twitter, Instagram, and Google searches), 35 percent of the time they find something that negatively affects an applicant's chances of being accepted.

The following exercise will present real-life examples of how teens present themselves on the Internet to help you think about your own online activity and what it says about you.

Exercise: Assess Your Online Persona

Read the following scenarios and answer three questions for each: What do you think is this person's intention? What might her parents think? And what might her crush think?

Example: A friend posts a picture of herself at the mall trying on swimsuits, with the comment "Hot or not?"

1. You think… *Wow, she really wants attention!*

2. Her parents think… *This is really inappropriate. We need to talk to her about this.*

3. Her crush thinks… *Cute, but why does she need to ask others if she's hot or not? She's probably insecure about her body. That's not attractive.*

A girl you know from school posts "OMG! I HATE *some* people! Why can't everyone just get lives and stop gossiping. LOSERS!"

1. You think…

2. Her parents think…

3. Her crush thinks…

Your best friend checks in constantly. Her news feed looks like a map of your town, and it's only 4 p.m. on a Saturday!

1. You think…

2. Her parents think…

3. Her crush thinks…

A girl on your feed always posts pictures of sad poems. Today, she posts a picture of a knife with the comment, "Maybe I'll spend the afternoon playing with this."

1.   You think…

2.   Her parents think…

3.   Her crush thinks…

Your friend is on vacation with her family and doesn't post any pictures until she gets home.

1.   You think…

2.   Her parents think…

3.   Her crush thinks…

A girl in your class makes a page dedicated to the teacher she hates.

1.   You think…

2.   Her parents think…

3.   Her crush thinks…

When you think about what these images and posts say about the person, do you notice that her intentions may not always be clear to others? That maybe other people will interpret what she thinks is cool as trying too hard? After thinking about it, are there changes you want to make to your own online presence? Maybe you'll reconsider allowing people to post hurtful comments on your blog, for example, because really, that's just like putting graffiti all over your locker—it's there for the whole school to see. And remember, the digital world is a billion times bigger than your school!

Director's Note

Evaluate the people in your life. Then promote, demote, or delete. You're the director of your life.

#ExpressYourself

Instant Gratification or Long-Term Problems

Snap, hashtag, post, like, share, ask, gram—you know the drill. All of these fun and exciting ways to connect on social media make it almost impossible to put your phone down. It can be cool to communicate with friends over # or @ signs, and fun to follow your favorite celebrities, peeking into their daily lives. Just remember that people are getting a view of yours as well.

You probably have a good idea of the potential consequences of sending a racy picture or responding rudely to a text. So if you know it might ultimately cost you your self-respect, what makes you feel like you should give in to the urge?

When your gadget is controlling you, you are not in control. But approaching your phone or keyboard with assertiveness requires you to do one thing your mind is not always good at: pressing the pause button. Adults have trouble with this too, but it's especially hard for teens. Why? Because the teenage brain has a hard time applying the brakes. You crave opportunities to bond with your buds, and after getting responses—including instant compliments—your brain continues to stay in overdrive. The only effective way to slow it down is to take mini breaks throughout the day. Put away your phone when you're at the table, doing your homework, or walking down the street. Live without the Internet for fifteen or twenty minutes.

Disconnecting, even for short periods of time, will help you practice self-control.

Here's another reason it's hard to resist the urge: anonymity. This is a funny thing. "Anonymity" means that people feel as if what they say or do online doesn't affect them, as if they are protected by their computer screen—but they're not. This is why so many people, even adults, say things online that they would never say in person. Being behind a screen gives people a sense of power while blinding them to the effects of their mean comments or of their desire for attention. Would you call your friend those names in a face-to-face interaction? Probably not. But words feel the same whether said online or in person. You can't take them back.

So how do you respond when your BFF sends you a rude message or your mom won't stop her steady stream of texts? How do you tap into your assertive mindset when your fingers are doing the talking? Well, in order to figure it out, you need to pause.

Your Rights

* You have the right to create, share, and express yourself online.

* You have the right to keep passwords and personal information private.

* You have the right to respond to messages online and through your phone when it's convenient for you.

* You have the right to make friends online, but you don't have to meet them in person.

87

* You have the right to unfriend, delete, and block people on social media.

* You have the right to refuse a friend request if you don't know the person or don't want to be friends with him or her online.

* You have the right to be treated with dignity and respect online—you can, and should, report users who do not treat you this way.

* You have the right to keep your personal information private—you don't have to share your journal, address, or pictures you don't want to go viral.

* You have the privilege of using technology. But it can be taken away if it's not used respectfully.

PAUSE Before You Post

Have you ever sent a text message in the heat of the moment, say when you were mad at someone, and then later looked at it and thought, *Wow that was actually kind of mean. I never would have said that in person*? You may have been embarrassed by your own behavior, ashamed, or even confused about what got into you. When you act impulsively, saying the first thing that comes to your mind, it's likely you'll end up wishing you had paused, perhaps editing it a little, before pressing send.

This chapter will show you how to use the acronym *PAUSE* to make sure you are respecting yourself and others before texting and posting, and to reduce your chances of saying something you'll later regret. This is a key component of being assertive. Think of the acronym as your own personal PR team. Here's what PAUSE stands for:

P: Put down the phone or the mouse for just a second.

A: Ask yourself what your intention—your desired result—is for what you're about to text or post. Is the intention a positive one or a negative one?

U: Urge surf. Just like a wave comes crashing down, an urge will lose its momentum if you give it a moment, and then you'll be able to think more clearly. (More on urge surfing in a second.)

S: Say it out loud. Other people will hear your comment as if it's in your voice. Try it with a mean tone and then with a nicer tone. Which way do you think it will be heard?

E: Edit. Before pressing send, make any changes you need to make to your message in order to be clearly understood. Add an emoticon to indicate your tone, delete words that are too forceful, or delete the whole message and start over.

Let's see how the PAUSE approach would work in a real-life situation.

Like everyone my age, I like to express my feelings online. If I'm upset or excited, I will post something in my status update about it or post a pic of something that represents how I'm feeling. Recently I've been posting quotes and song lyrics about being a true friend and about how actions speak louder than words. The truth is, my best friend broke my trust, and we're no longer on speaking terms. But now other people think my updates are about them, and it's causing a lot of drama. How can I express my feelings without all the drama?

It's not unusual for teens to use status updates as a tool for self-disclosure ("OMG WORST CRAMPS EVER") or as a way of tossing out a not-so-subtle hint ("I wish SOMEONE would call me back..."). Although it may seem assertive to say how you feel online, it can sometimes be more passive-aggressive and do more harm than good.

True assertiveness would be telling your friend how you feel, rather than posting quotes and song lyrics that only hint at it. What's not being directly expressed here is "I'm hurt" or "I want an apology," and this kind of thing really should be said in person, so you know that it's being heard. Sure, typing or texting is easier to do, and it can be a good way to let someone know you'd like to talk and set up a time. As you know, text messages on emotional topics can easily be misunderstood, and those doing the texting can easily fall into the trap of saying mean things. Plus, having to wait for your friend's responses can cause a lot of unneeded anxiety.

So here's where you PAUSE:

P: Put down the phone or the mouse.

A: Ask yourself what your intention is for posting the quotes and song lyrics. Are you trying to get her to see that you're really hurt? What if she doesn't see your page? How will she know? If she does see the page, how do you think she'll interpret it?

U: Urge surf. Alan Marlatt, author and professor of psychology, came up with the phrase "urge surf." Since urges are just like waves, the emotions can be intense, and they can peak, but they eventually crash. Your urge won't last forever, and the last thing you want to do is press send when you're at the peak of frustration or any intense feeling. Acknowledge your desire to post whatever it is you feel like posting, but don't do it yet. Allow some time for the intensity to pass so you can think more clearly. Distract yourself by doing something else just for a minute. Play a game on your phone; call another friend; write in your journal; do something else for now. Give the "wave" time to lose its momentum and crash.

S: Say out loud what you want to say or write to your friend, and listen to how it sounds. How would other people hear it? Would it sound kind, or would it sound mean? Is there a chance that, if she reads it, she might hear your rude tone of voice—you know the one you use when you are complaining or angry with someone? Say what you're thinking of writing out loud in an aggressive or rude tone of voice, then say it with your sweet and sincere voice. If they sound the same, then you're good to post, but if you notice your mean voice makes your message sound rude, rethink it.

E: Edit. If you still feel that it's a good idea to post what you wanted to post, could you change your language in some way so that it's less likely to be misinterpreted or more likely to have a positive impact?

To Send or Not to Send?

Even if you follow the steps of PAUSE and it's past the impulsive stage, it can still be hard to make a decision about sending a text or picture. It may seem like a great idea at first, but will you regret it later? Looking at the big picture—all the possible pros and cons, both short-term and long-term—can help you determine whether it's a good idea.

For example, say you have the urge to send a flirty text and a suggestive photo to your new crush. Your two choices are to send or not to send. One way you could approach this decision is to take out a piece of paper and make a chart that looks something like this:

Pros of Sending It

* He may like me more.
* He may want me to be his girlfriend.
* I look pretty.
* It's exciting.

Cons of Sending It

* His parents could see it.
* He may not delete it.
* I could get in trouble.
* I might feel embarrassed afterward.
* He may like or respect me less.

Pros of Not Sending It

* I won't have to worry about my picture floating around.
* I won't have to worry about my parents or his parents seeing it.
* I won't lose respect.

Cons of Not Sending It

* I won't have the fun and excitement of sending it.
* He may not know I'm interested.
* He may lose interest.

After you've finished your chart, go back and indicate which of these feelings or consequences are short-term (ST), meaning they'll last no longer than a day or two, and which are long-term (LT), meaning they could last weeks, months, or years.

Pros of Sending It

* He may like me more. (LT)

* He may want me to be his girlfriend. (LT)

* I look pretty. (ST)

* It's exciting. (ST)

Cons of Sending It

* His parents could see it. (ST)

* He may not delete it. (LT)

* I could get in trouble. (LT)

* I might feel embarrassed afterward. (ST)

* He may like or respect me less. (LT)

Pros of Not Sending It

* I won't have to worry about my picture floating around. (LT)

* I won't have to worry about my parents or his parents seeing it. (LT)

* I won't lose respect. (LT)

Cons of Not Sending It

* I won't have the fun and excitement of sending it. (ST)

* He may not know I'm interested. (ST)

* He may lose interest. (LT)

If you still can't decide, count up which decision has the most long-term consequences—the ones that could stick with you forever. Then decide if it's worth it.

Learn Your Lines

Let's move on to some common situations that teens encounter
in their daily lives. The scenarios presented in the rest of this
chapter include scripts for how to handle specific conflicts that
can arise in online communication. You can memorize the lines
you like or use the scripts as a starting point for improvising
your own lines when you encounter similar situations.

The Situation: Friends Online, Invisible in Person

*I chat online every night with a popular girl at school. We
follow each other on social media sites, complain about
teachers we have at school, and attempt to help each other
with homework. I think that we're getting closer, but at
school she barely acknowledges my existence. Whenever I ask
her to hang out off-line she makes an excuse, but then I see
pictures or posts about other friends she's been hanging with.
It hurts my feelings. Why won't she be friends with me in
person?*

Communicating online is often easier than in person. Obviously, she likes you and wants to be friends. Otherwise, why chat with you? Actually, there are two possibilities here: either she's not aware of how you feel, or she's too enslaved to the rules of her group to connect with someone on the outside. Whatever the reason, she's blowing you off, and so far, you're putting up with it.

When you allow someone to be your friend only on her terms, you teach her that it's okay to treat you like a doormat. "I'm here whenever you need me," is not the most self-respecting way to set the terms for a friendship, and it's not what you do when you want to be in charge of your own life. Do movie directors hire actors who work only when they want to? No, because they need dependable people—and so do you.

Before You Say a Word

If you don't have a very strong off-line relationship yet, it can feel awkward to express yourself like we did in chapter 2. But you can make a point with your behavior. If your goal is to see whether this relationship is worthy of your time, then test the waters. If your goal is to get her to become your BFF, be careful. Coming on too strong or too needy can be felt even across the Internet. If you're always available, she doesn't have a chance to realize how much you mean to her. Even if you're sitting at the computer waiting for her to log on, try to behave in a way that sends a message that you're not available for her all the time. This may sound like playing games, but it's really a way to let her know you value yourself and your time.

Set the Scene

Experiment with availability. Next time she contacts you, take a little longer to respond, or be unavailable at the time you two usually start chatting. Limit the time you spend talking to her. Have a few phrases ready for when she messages you that let her know you want to be friendly, but you've also got other things to do: "Hey, swamped with HW SRY super busy TTYL." Add an emoticon for added friendliness if you feel it's too harsh.

What to Say

You obviously have to speak up sometime or it will be a very draining relationship. You might want to give it a little time to see if her behavior changes once she realizes that you're not interested in a one-way friendship. If you feel like she hasn't got the message or things aren't changing, then try the sandwich technique.

> **Bread (positive statement):** *It's fun talking to you online and doing our homework together (or avoiding it LOL).*

> **Peanut butter (request):** *I know we're both busy, but I think it would be really fun to hang out sometime off-line. Maybe at lunch or after school? Let me know when you're free.*

> **Bread (positive statement):** *Hope to see you soon!* ☺

The message you're sending is that you respect yourself and you take your relationships seriously. You don't want a part-time friend; you want a friend who acknowledges you online *and* in person.

What to Do When...

What if she doesn't come running to hang out with her fabulously assertive online friend? Like it or not, the reality is that online communication doesn't always translate to true friendship. So think about it this way: you've just spared yourself any further attachment to a person who's not treating you well. Both friends and romantic interests who prefer online-only relationships can make you feel like you're not good enough—when in fact you are awesome, and they are missing out. You might be thinking, *Well, I'd rather have some attention than none.* But putting up with that kind of disrespect is like putting up with a diva on the set of your movie—the one who's always arriving late, expecting special treatment, and trying to dictate the script. It's for you to decide whether you want to treat yourself with respect by setting boundaries around friends who don't give you as much as you give them—online or off-line. Remember, no one can take advantage of you if you don't allow it.

Reflection Questions: Have you ever been in a friendship or relationship like this, either the invisible friend or the one doing the ignoring? How did you feel? How did you handle it? How would you prevent it from happening again? What would you say or do?

The Situation: Pressure to Pose

I really like this guy at school. He and I have been hanging out a lot and texting constantly. A few weeks ago, we were video chatting and he asked me to get undressed. I made up an excuse—that I didn't have a lock on my door. Now he keeps asking me to send him pictures of myself, without clothes. I don't know if I want to, but I'm afraid if I don't he will stop liking me. I can't tell if I'm being a prude or if I'm being pressured.

First of all, bravo for coming up with an excuse to avoid doing something risky online—you might have regretted it later. You listened to your intuition and your self-respect, which is hard to do when there's pressure to please someone else. Whenever you give in to pressure, you're essentially letting someone else steal the spotlight—you give in and you lose some of your directing power, that confidence you've been working so hard to achieve! This makes it far more difficult to assert yourself in the future, as well as making you feel less secure and more anxious. You can't be 100 percent sure that info you share will stay with the person it's intended for, and that leads to freaky feelings. As you learned in chapter 1, the more your emotions are running on high, the less likely you are able to feel confident and assert yourself in any situation, especially with this dude.

The truth is that the way a guy or girl treats you online isn't much different than how he or she treats you in person. So you have to ask yourself: Do I want a relationship with someone who would keep pressuring me to do something I'm clearly not comfortable with?

Before You Say a Word

First, consider these facts:

* Studies show that about one-third of the pictures that are texted or sent online and intended to be private are shared with friends or forwarded to others—yikes!

* If you are under eighteen (seventeen in some states), receiving nude or semi-nude pictures is considered possession of child pornography.

* Parents can be charged with a crime and jailed for their kids' sexting activity. The phones are often in the parents' names, and they have ultimate responsibility for electronic use within the household. So they face a big risk if you are involved in any of the following:

  * possession of a picture that is considered child pornography, even if you're not in the picture

  * sending this kind of photo—which can be considered promoting child pornography and can have legal consequences, even if it's sent only to that special someone

  * distribution (sharing) of a photo—which is why, if someone sends one to you, you should delete it and never forward it

Set the Scene

Regardless of the potential legal issues, it sounds like you aren't entirely comfortable sending a picture of yourself. The way you approach this situation will depend on how comfortable you are with this guy. So ask yourself the following questions:

1. Do you feel like you could tell him the truth about why you don't think it's a good idea?

2. Are you afraid that he will up the ante and keep pressuring you, making it harder to say no?

3. Do you feel like you want to say no, but you don't know how?

The script you choose will be based on your answers.

What to Say

Review these assertive lines to see which ones best fit your situation and your personality:

* *I'm not into sharing stuff like that.*

* *I might be open to it in person, but not online. That's never turned out well for anyone I know.*

* *You might be okay with the risks, but I'm not.*

* *Nice try, but I'm not willing to have my private pictures out in the digital universe forever.*

* *No way. Spyware is everywhere, and I don't want my parents seeing stuff like that.*

* *I'm sure you'd keep them private, but I don't trust the Internet.*

* *I'm not that kind of girl.* (Can be said in a humorous way.)

All of these responses show that you respect yourself, and the way he responds will show whether he respects you too. If he doesn't, then he could very well be the type who would share your pictures with others without your consent.

What to Do When...

What if he gets mad or stops talking to you? That's the main fear that many girls have when deciding whether to stand up for themselves—that they will lose a friend or a potential romantic partner. Instead of giving in or getting upset, ask yourself whether someone like this is really a friend or someone you would want to date. He's already disrespecting you by pressuring you to do something you're not comfortable with and something that could have serious consequences for both of you.

Reflection Questions: Have you ever thought about what would happen if you sent a text, picture, or video and it got into the wrong hands? What would you do?

Have you had friends who have sent or received pictures or inappropriate content? What happened? Do you think they kept it to themselves or showed their friends?

What would you do if you received a picture like that? How would it make you feel?

Write Your Script: Now it's your turn. Think about if you were in this situation, and write a script using the PAUSE skill in your journal.

Been There, Done That—Advice from Women Who've Been in Your Shoes

Jaime Gleicher, MA, LMSW, is a psychotherapist and former MTV reality star.

Over ten years ago, I was a "reality TV star," a title that has followed me into my professional life. When I was seventeen and a senior in high school, I was given the opportunity to create, produce, and star in a reality television show for MTV. In the end, the product was a lot different than I had intended it to be. That's show business. When the show came out, it got a lot of press; all of which ended up online. If you Googled me, you saw that not only was I defined as a "rich girl," a label they gave me, I was the victim of relentless online bullying, calling me fat and ugly. I realized that fame was actually not glamorous but rather painful. I made the choice to leave that lifestyle behind, but my online reputation still haunts me to this day.

Even after embarking on a courageous career as a psychotherapist so I could help other young girls create their own positive life paths, the digital footprint still remains. I still have to explain myself to potential employers, clients, professors, and peers who Google me and find out about my past as a "reality television star." I am proof that in today's society everything ends up online. As I tried to create a new identity for myself, I realized how deep the imprint of my previous life choices were. The only solution was to acknowledge and accept that I had made choices that could not be erased while also realizing that I could

102

create new footprints. I chose, and continuously choose, to make these footprints that are meaningful and reflective of who I am now, which includes raising mental health awareness. In a world where we can't delete everything online, the one thing we can do is to choose to control what does get out there.

The Situation: I'm Being Cyberbullied

Until last year, I was part of "the clique." Then the guy that my best friend had a crush on started liking me. I guess she got mad because now all the girls from the clique tease me online and at school. They've recently been posting embarrassing pictures of me from middle school and adding hurtful images and words like "slut" to them. When I asked them to stop, they said if I told on them, they'd make my life even worse. I don't want to talk to my parents because they might think I did something wrong too. I'm sick of feeling this way, but I don't know what to do.

It's understandable that you are hurt and embarrassed—maybe even scared. They may have been your friends at one point, but they aren't now. What they're doing is not just disrespectful and hurtful—they're bullying you.

In a situation like this, it can be hard to figure out what to do or whom to tell. Will your mom think you're a slut? Will your teacher talk to the parents of these girls, leading to even more bullying? These are the common fears that can keep you from speaking up and getting help.

Before You Say a Word

You are not alone. In fact, there are so many teens who have been in your shoes that now there are websites, support lines, and even texting lines that can help you if you are afraid to talk to an adult in your life. Here are some questions to ask yourself that will help you figure out what to do:

1. Is there an adult in my life whom I can go to for help—a teacher, counselor, parent, friend, or coach?

2. What is the worst that could happen if I talk to one of these adults?

3. What if these girls hate me? Would I want to be friends with people like them anyway?

4. If I don't speak up, will they continue doing things like this to other people? What if they bully someone who is really sensitive and cause serious distress or even suicide?

Set the Scene

While you're figuring out what to do or say, save everything! You may need it later as evidence. Take screen shots with your phone or on your computer. Don't delete any texts or e-mails. If they harass you in person, write down the things they say, including dates and times.

What to Say

There are several different ways you could approach this scene. Some involve more assertiveness than others. You're the director, so see which one feels right to you, and if needed, adapt it in your own words if that feels more comfortable.

1. Ask them to stop: "I know you don't like me, but can you please stop posting these things. If you have something to say to me, you can say it in person and we can just move on with our lives." You can say this by text, or face-to-face with the other person. Yes, it might be embarrassing if they yell at you or say mean things in public. On the other hand, other people will be witnesses to their terrible behavior—they will likely look at them negatively, not you. If they respond with something rude or insulting, you've got proof to show those adults who will help you get them to stop.

2. Talk to a trusted adult. You can do this by phone, e-mail, or in person. Share your evidence. Show it to the adult on your device, and consider printing the evidence out to keep a record of the bullying. Let the adult know whether you want to remain anonymous. (If what you're showing this person is all over social media, then anyone could turn the bullies in.) If you feel you need protection, let the adult know that.

3. Have your parents call the principal and set up a time for a face-to-face meeting. Most schools have a zero-tolerance policy for this kind of harassment. The principal and

your parents can also help figure out whether to involve law enforcement or inform the Internet service provider.

However you choose to deal with this situation, there could be some backlash. They may know it's you who told, but you have to be brave. Act confident, self-assured, and above all else, let it pass. This may seem like the worst thing ever and the biggest news since that famous reality TV star got married—again! Don't worry—it will pass faster than her first marriage, or even the two-hour special you saw on TV, and this is no different. Like any celebrity headline, which loses its buzz within a few days, your drama will be old news soon enough. The less of a reaction you give to your bullies and the audience looking on, the faster it will go away. And the more attention you give them in your interactions or reactions (tears, threats, even the evil eye in the hallway), the more you are showing them they affect you. Just like in chapter 3, you want to teach them to change their behavior, and you do this by not giving them an ounce of your power.

Do *not* perpetuate the problem by responding online to the bullying messages. Doing so could get you into trouble, even if your intention is to stop it. Don't ruin your case by calling them names or running your mouth to the wrong people. If you want to talk to friends about what's going on, do it in person.

The bottom line is that the bullying will likely stop when you take a stand. As uncomfortable as it might be to confront the bullies or talk to an adult about it, think of how much worse you'll feel if you sacrifice your self-respect and let them get away with their behavior. Remember, it's your movie—you don't want to give others the role of director.

What to Do When...

Change of scene: What do you do when you're in a situation in which you might be part of the problem, possibly one of the bullies? What if you're a bystander, watching this happening to someone you know? Or what if it's your friends who are doing the harassing and you do nothing to stop it? If so, you could be considered part of the bullying.

Studies have shown that 95 percent of teen Internet users have witnessed bullying on social media, and 55 percent say they witness it frequently. Even worse, 66 percent of teens say they've witnessed others joining in on the bullying, and 21 percent admit to jumping on the bandwagon. An alarming number of teens—90 percent—have witnessed bullying but chosen to ignore it.

The reality is that if you're forwarding, commenting, or liking, or if you're in a group message, you could possibly get in serious trouble. So what do you do? It can be hard to stand up to mean or powerful people and even harder if you're friends with them. Nobody wants to feel like a social outcast. Here are some things you can say or do to escape the bystander role:

* "I don't want to get in trouble; don't put my name on it."

* "I have to go. I forgot I have _____." (Come up with an excuse to leave the situation if you don't know what to do or say.)

* "Guys, we could get in serious trouble. I don't know about you, but I don't want that to happen."

* "Leave me out of this. It's bullying."

107

Consider doing something more active and helpful than excusing yourself. Think about it: What if the victim of this bullying ends up being one of those people who tries to hurt or kill herself as a result? Will you feel guilty for not speaking up? As a bystander, you have more power than you think. You can make an anonymous report through a website or to your school principal, for example. The important thing is that you act according to your conscience. Listen to your gut and make yourself proud.

Reflection Questions: Have you seen someone get bullied or harassed online? How did it feel to watch this person's reputation become tarnished?

What would you do or say if you saw one of your friends cyberbullying someone? What would keep you from speaking up?

What would you do if one of your friends was the victim? How would you help her?

The Situation: Confusing Communication

My friends constantly misinterpret my texts. Just recently I said I couldn't hang out after school (because I had a makeup test). They took that as rude, and now they're not talking to me. I tried to call them, but everyone ignored me. It's so frustrating because I can't ever get them on the phone to talk it out!

You are not alone. Millions of people experience this kind of misunderstanding—adults too! It happens often when people communicate by text, chat, or e-mail. Your communication probably went something like this:

Group Text: Meet @ coffee shop L8R B there!

Me: Cant sry

Group Text: WTF U too good for us now?

Me: What???!

Me: I have a test I have to make up & then HW. SRY.

Group Text: Whatever

Within minutes you go from feeling connected to your group to feeling completely dissed. The problem is that tone is hard to decipher when you can't hear someone's voice. So when texting, you might have to do a little extra work to get others to understand what you're really trying to say.

Before You Say a Word

If you're upset by a text message, take a moment before replying. Review the steps of PAUSE outlined earlier in this chapter. What are you trying to do here? You're trying to clear up the confusion, right? This is best done by talking it out off-line—in person or on the phone.

Set the Scene

As you may have noticed, to get people to see your point of view, you sometimes have to give a little first. Owning up to your part in the misunderstanding can lower their defenses and make them more willing to talk with you on the phone or in person. So before you talk to your friends, ask yourself, "Did I have any part in this problem?" See if you can understand how they may have interpreted your comments as not so nice. Then use this understanding to your advantage.

What to Say

Owning up can be hard, especially when your feelings are hurt. If your goal is to patch things up, you'll find it will help to ask yourself how they may have "heard" your message. Try a little empathy, just like you learned in chapter 3. Text something like, "Hey, sorry I was so short earlier in my text. I didn't mean to sound rude. I'm just super busy. I would love to hang out soon. Let's talk tomorrow at lunch. Miss you! Xoxo."

In other words, explain what happened and apologize for any misunderstanding. It shouldn't take more than three sentences. Save the long-winded explanations for an in-person chat. If they don't respond immediately and positively to your text, try not to sweat it. You did the best you could, and you were respectful to both yourself and them.

Avoid Texting Mishaps

Mistakes and misinterpretation can come from feeling the urge to instantly respond, typing too fast, or assuming your receiver knows what you are trying to say. It happens all the time and can be avoided by following some of these assertiveness texting and typing tips.

* Short answers are often misinterpreted. "K" or "?" leaves too much room for interpretation. Try "Okay sounds good" instead, or "I don't understand, can you explain?" It takes about ten seconds more to type and gives you control over the message you are sending.

* Give yourself time to respond. Turn off read receipts telling other people that the texts have been seen. These receipts create anxiety and pressure to respond rapidly and invites them to interpret your delay as something it's not. Avoid the "why aren't you responding" fight. It's your life, talk or text on your terms.

* Don't "YELL." Avoid all capital letters. It feels like you are aggressive or angry. "CALL ME BACK," even if you are excited, sends the wrong message. Try instead, "Call me back when you can," and add a smiley face.

* Send the right text to the right person. Have you ever sent an e-mail or text in a hurry and sent it to the wrong person or worse yet, to the person you didn't want to read it? Talk about awkward. Take 2.2 seconds to make sure it's headed to the right person.

* Avoid autocorrect drama. You know how embarrassing it can be when you intended to type "that's crazy" and it turns into "my legs are hairy" or

something totally unrelated to your texting convo. Prevent the phone from communicating for you by taking a moment to read a message over before pressing send.

* Use your manners. Even though you're not at the dinner table, saying please and thank you does help get your message across. "Meet me after school" sounds bossy, but "Could you please meet me after school today?" sounds much more like a request than a demand.

When in doubt, take the conversation off-line and pick up the phone. Your conversation will be heard, not just interpreted, which will make you feel much more assured about the message you are sending to others.

What to Do When...

What if your friends won't talk off-line and keep texting hurtful things—even after you apologized? You might be tempted to continue texting, but think about whether you really want to leave a text trail of your feelings saved on someone's phone. Remember, you never know who else might be looking at that phone. The idea here is to talk with your actual voices. It can be video chat, in person, or on the phone. Repeat your request nicely: "I'd really like to talk this out in person."

Reflection Questions: Have you ever been on the receiving end of a texting mishap? Did you get upset or lose your cool over an assumption? How did you handle it?

If that situation were to occur again in the future, what would you say or do?

Before Logging Off...

The many situations discussed in this chapter are examples of how complex and challenging online communication can be. Hopefully they've highlighted the fact that it's just as important to stand up for yourself in the virtual world as it is in real life.

Speaking of real life, in the next chapter we'll log off and focus on how to be yourself while being with your crowd—including strategies for dealing with peer pressure, parties, and romantic relationships.

Be the person your future self will thank you for—not hate you for.

Director's Note

PAUSE before you post (or press Send).

#ExpressYourself

Chapter 5

The Social Butterfly: You with Your Peers

The comfort in knowing that you are being your full self, or if you don't know who that is, just doing what feels right in the moment, will triumph over the comfort of knowing that some hypothetical other person is into a boring, pretty, one-dimensional version of you that doesn't exist.

— Tavi Gevinson, Editor-in-Chief, Rookie, http://www.rookiemag.com

As a teen, you're faced with temptations almost every day to do things you may not be comfortable with. Do any of these situations sound familiar? A girl in the bathroom offers you one of her prescription pills to help you concentrate during midterms; a friend who smokes cigarettes hands you one when you're stressed out about school; your crush offers you a ride home, but you've promised your parents you won't get in a car with someone they don't know. These situations wouldn't be much of a problem if it weren't for the fact that part of you is curious and tempted to go against your better judgment.

Peer pressure—social pressure by friends, classmates, cliques, and other peer groups to conform to the group's norms or expectations—can have a strong influence on decision making. People often give in to peer pressure because they're afraid of being teased and rejected or because they are kind of curious about what an experience will be like. Going along with it might seem like the only choice if you want to maintain your friendships and your social status—but it doesn't have to be.

Even when you're confident that you know the right thing to do, there can be a strong pull to do something more risky, exciting, or even dangerous. Why not, right? All of your friends have done it. The desire to fit in or feel grown-up can drive you to make decisions that may seem fun in the moment but that don't align with who you are or who you want to be. Don't worry—this chapter isn't a parenting lecture or a sugarcoated talk about drugs and alcohol. It's a guide to understanding how peer pressure affects you, and it will arm you with effective ways to handle it without feeling awkward.

Who Influences You?

No matter which school you go to, which mall you shop in, or which friends you choose to hang out with, you face some of the same pressures and decisions that teens everywhere have to deal with, and the same bottom line: Are you going to do something you'll regret or respect? Remember it's your movie and you're the director. Impulsive decisions could result in hiring the wrong cast or crew members, cutting crucial scenes in the editing process, or creating a soundtrack that really doesn't go with the story you're trying to tell. Letting your peers run the show messes with your confidence and your vision and can make it much harder, if not impossible, for you to make a movie you'll be proud of in the end.

There's nothing wrong with allowing others to have influence. After all, just about every decision you've made—how you dress, the music you listen to, the clubs or activities you're involved in—has been influenced by your family, your friends, the community you live in, or advertising and media. Allowing yourself to be influenced isn't necessarily a bad thing. But don't forget life gives you the opportunity to reinvent yourself as your interests change. For example, as a kid maybe you loved a certain star from the Disney Channel. As you've grown up and been exposed to new things and new people, you probably took down your posters of that TV star and replaced them with, say, a new favorite band.

Problems with Peer Pressure

The influence itself is not the problem—it's the pressure that can sometimes go along with it. Everyone has felt peer pressure at some point. Remember back in elementary school, when you had to get that bracelet that all the girls had (even though you didn't really like it)? You may have gone as far as begging and pleading with your parents to buy you the bracelet because you *had* to have it. That kind of pressure doesn't go away, even when you're an adult. But the ability to identify pressure, know what it feels like, and act according to what you truly want changes as you grow up—it also helps you feel confident and comfortable in the skin you're in. The older you get, the clearer you get about who you are and what you stand for, and the easier it gets to assert yourself in ways that align your decisions with your values.

116

Director's Note

When you give in to others, you give away
your power. Stay true to you.

#ExpressYourself

Unspoken Pressure

Peer pressure is not always obvious. The ways your friends—or even celebrities—talk, act, or dress can rub off on you without your even knowing. Unspoken pressure is trickier because it's not someone telling you what to do—it's unsaid. The pressure is based on a feeling or a desire to be cool or fit in. Unspoken pressure is especially hard to resist because instead of standing up to a friend, you have to stand up to your own feelings.

Of course, unspoken pressure can sometimes have a positive effect. For example, if your friends make fun of the girls who smoke after school, it makes it easier to say no when someone offers you a puff. You care what your friends think, and you don't want them to make fun of you. Often, unspoken pressure causes teens to go against their better judgment, especially in FOMO (fear of missing out) situations. Say you missed the last party and saw pictures that were posted, making you wish you had gone. Everyone was talking about it for weeks! So the next time, you go even though you don't really want to. Your urge to party comes from your feeling that everyone else is partying, and you don't want to miss out—even if it winds up a disaster, or gets you in trouble.

Reflection Questions: How are you influenced by unspoken pressure? Do particular celebrities, TV shows, or people in your life make you to feel like you need to dress, look, or act a certain way?

Have you ever bought makeup or another product because you loved the celebrity in the ad? Think of the last thing you purchased. Who influenced this decision? A friend? A parent? A celebrity?

Have you ever caved in to unspoken pressure from friends? What did you do? How did you feel afterward?

Think of a time when you experienced positive unspoken peer pressure. What was the situation? How did you feel?

Spoken Pressure

Sometimes you know that "everyone is doing it" because they're telling you they are! Spoken pressure is direct: "You're the only one in our group of friends who hasn't had sex. Everyone else is ditching school. How come you never want to smoke pot with us?" It may be that they're not exactly telling you *what* to do, but they're making you feel bad about yourself because you're not doing whatever it is they think is cool.

When friends use spoken pressure, it's a clear sign that they don't care about your values, your bottom line, or the movie you're trying to make. Sure, they like to hang with you, but they're not concerned about whether you feel comfortable—or whether you get grounded for the rest of your life. They care about themselves, the moment, and having their kind of fun, no matter how you feel about it. Here's one girl's experience with spoken pressure:

Claire hung out with some of the "popular" kids, upperclassmen whom she thought of as cool and who were always inviting her to parties. When Claire got the part-time job of her dreams at her favorite boutique, it meant waking up at 8 a.m. on weekends to open the shop. Every Friday when there was a party, her friends gave her a hard time about leaving before they did. "Don't be lame—it's early," they'd say, or, "We thought you were cool. Only losers go home before midnight."

These friends didn't seem to care that she was trying to be responsible and prioritize her job. But Claire knew if she were to stay out too late, she would risk oversleeping and maybe getting fired. Eventually she caved and stayed out late. She set three alarms, but she still overslept, and guess what? She was late for work. Her boss gave her a warning and said if she was late again, she would be fired. Her boss was not the only one who was unhappy. Claire was disappointed in herself as well. It was a feeling that stuck with her for a long time.

Reflection Questions: In your opinion, were the extra couple of hours with her friends worth the consequences?

What would you have done if you were in Claire's shoes? What would you say to your friends?

Are there people in your life that are like Claire's crew? If so, how do you feel when you are around them?

Have you ever been in a situation where you told your friends to lay off? What did you say and how did it make you feel?

Remember, the director, not the cast, runs the show. If you let others take that power, your film will be a disaster. You're the expert in your own life—you live in your head every day, and you're the one who lives with the consequences of your decisions.

Your Rights

* You have the right to say no.

* You have the right to be angry or upset.

* You have the right to not accept responsibility for others' behavior, feelings, or problems.

* You have the right to respectfully disagree.

* You have the right to put your own needs ahead of your peers'.

* You have the right to make decisions based on values or gut feelings, without having to give reasons.

* You have the right to be treated with respect by your peers.

* You have the right to remove yourself from situations you don't want to be in.

Simple Ways to Say "No Thanks"

Saying no isn't something that most people find easy to do. In situations where the goal is to maintain your friendships without compromising your values, it can be really tricky. The key is being true to yourself while being respectful to your friends, even when you don't agree with them. If you're not used to saying no, it may feel weird at first. Just remember, "no" doesn't mean you're arguing. It's just expressing yourself in the moment.

Here are some general rules to follow when dealing with pushy people or situations in which you're feeling pressured:

* Be unapologetic. Saying that you're sorry for being yourself gives the impression that you're insecure. It also makes others think that you're not totally sure about your decision and invites them to keep pushing. Which would you respect more: "Sorry, I just don't think I can," or "I'm not into it, but thanks for the invite"?

* Don't argue with the pressure—try to understand it instead. Why would your friends be pressuring you to do something you don't want to do? Maybe they're unsure about their own decisions or afraid of being judged. See if you can find a piece of empathy for them. It could be that they are driven by their own fears or lack of confidence.

* Instead of arguing with other people's decisions, just listen and nod before saying anything. It sends the message that you aren't judging or disapproving (even if you are), and it makes it easier for them to accept your "no."

* Use excuses in moderation. Be brief and to the point when you give a reason for declining.

The "Both/And" Technique

People often forget that in any disagreement, both people can be right. It's always a good idea to acknowledge that. Say something like, "You're right, it seems fun—and I'd rather not." (Using *and* instead of *but* can help prevent defensiveness.)

There are many other ways to say "no thanks" and show that you mean it:

* "I can't."

* "You know me; that's not my style."

* "Not my thing."

* "Nah. You guys have fun, though."

* "Let's try to hang out some other time."

Here's an example of how the "both/and" technique can work with pushy peers:

Peers: Hey, skip class with us—we're going to smoke. Plus that super-hot senior I told you about is going to be there. You have to come!

You: That sounds really fun. I've got to be in class, though. My teacher's really strict about attendance. Can I meet him another time?

Peers: You are such a baby. Relax, your teacher won't care.

You: I can see why it seems that way, and I'm trying to get my GPA up. I can't risk it. Let's hang out after school or something.

When you are able to express yourself without being judgmental, saying no shouldn't hurt your relationships. Even if you don't agree with your friends' behavior, they will be glad not to have to defend it.

Learn Your Lines

Let's move on to some situations that are commonly encountered by teen girls. The scenarios in the rest of this chapter present tricky situations and possible ways to approach the dialogue. You can follow these scripts or improvise if you like. If the situations don't ring true for you, think about how you would use the skills in a situation you have actually encountered.

The Situation: I'm About to Cave!

All my friends are hooking up and getting wasted on the weekends. They have morphed from the girls who used to have sleepovers to the girls who sneak out, smoke pot, and sleep around. They make me feel like a goody-two-shoes because I don't do these things. They say I should live a little, dress hotter, and stop being a prude. I'm not the type to crumble under peer pressure, but I'm starting to feel like a loser. My so-called friends are leaving me off group texts and not inviting me to hang out. Even though I don't agree with what they're doing, I'm envious because they all seem to be having so much fun. Maybe I really should live a little. I just don't know what to do!

Peer pressure is the worst, especially when it comes from your friends. You may even be questioning why you're hanging out with these people at all. If you're not comfortable with the idea of getting high, hooking up, or engaging in other risky behaviors that your friends are doing, that's a good thing. It's your intuition telling you that it's probably not in your best interest. It's too bad that you should have to explain this—and defend it—to the people you consider to be your crew. If they're going to make you feel bad about that, then honestly, they aren't really good friends.

Making choices that are different from those of your friends doesn't mean there's something wrong with you. There are a lot of girls and guys out there who would respect you for saying "no thanks" to all those activities (some of which are illegal). At the same time, it sounds like you do want to maintain these friendships, so your challenge is to find a balance between being yourself and being part of the group—that doesn't mean giving in.

Before You Say a Word

It's hard to assert yourself before you're clear about what you want. So ask yourself what your goal is. Here it sounds as if you want to keep your friends and keep your self-respect. You may be interested in trying out some of the things your friends are doing. But before you make a decision, sit for a moment and listen to your gut.

Actors often do warm-ups before stepping on set. These exercises help them get into character, focus on the scene, and remember their lines. Here's a suggestion for a warm-up before having a conversation with your friends:

Start by sitting quietly for a minute. Inhale for five counts, hold for five counts, and then exhale for five counts. Do this a few times, focusing on your breath. Then tune in to your inner guide. "Your inner guide" is a term that happiness guru Gabrielle Bernstein uses to describe your intuition, we don't always hear it when we aren't tuning into it. It's basically your "gut feeling"—that little voice that calls to you when you're about to walk down a dark alley, get in the car with a drunk driver, or peek at your classmate's paper during an exam: "Don't do it, girl!" We all ignore that inner guide from time to time, but generally she's right. And going against your gut feeling can often lead to trouble.

After you've sat and tuned in for a few minutes, let your mind run to the what-ifs of the situation. There's no way to know exactly what will happen if you sneak out, hook up with someone, or take a hit from a joint, but try to imagine the possibilities.

* First, imagine how you will feel about your behavior the next day. When you reflect on whatever you did the night before, do you think you will feel good about yourself?

* Then imagine how you'll feel a few months later. Looking back on your actions, do you think you might regret what you did? Will you have less respect for yourself? Will you wish you had stuck to your own moral code?

* Imagine where your friends will be a year or two from now. Do you think they'll have good relationships with their parents and teachers? Will they be respected by their peers?

* How do your friends appear in the eyes of others? Will your reputation be compromised if you give in?

Say you've used the warm-up exercise, and you're clear about what you want, but the thought of asking for it still stresses you out. This list of tips may help keep stress from making you give in to the quick fix instead of finding a healthier solution.

* Take time to chill out. Read a good book, make time for a hobby like cooking or painting, spend time with your pet, take a relaxing bath, or do something that you enjoyed as a little girl.

* Avoid avoiding. Have a big project or task you've been putting off? Take one small step toward getting started. The more you avoid, the bigger the stressor becomes.

* Ask for help. Have you bitten off more than you can chew? Then get brave and honest, and ask an adult, friend, or classmate for a little help. People like helping, and it makes them feel good too.

* Be of service. When you help someone, it helps you too. Helping your sibling with homework, running an errand for Mom, going through your closet and donating clothes to charity—all of these can take just a few minutes and help you tap into a positive mindset, which reduces stress.

* Be realistic. Don't try to be perfect—no one is. And expecting others to be perfect can add to your stress level. Understand that people may mess up and remind yourself that you are doing the best you can.

* Get grateful. This can help you get out of the stressful mindset you're stuck in and create a more compassionate and calm attitude. Think of as many things to be thankful for as you can for a minute or two.

* Get enough rest. The biological "sleep clock" shifts during adolescence. Many teens prefer staying up a little later at night and sleeping a little later in the morning, meaning you may not get enough sleep. Getting enough sleep is important because your batteries need to recharge.

* Zen out. Your brain needs to chill, but sometimes it's impossible turn off the stressful chatter in your mind. Try a guided meditation or relaxation for a few minutes. Gabrielle Bernstein has some guided mediations that can help you stress less in as little as two minutes online at http://www.gabbyb.tv/meditate.

Keep in mind that you can use these tips to fight stress in all kinds of situations, not just with peers who pressure you.

Set the Scene

Any time your goal is to salvage a relationship, you've got to find some empathy. Ask yourself why your friends are trying so hard to make you different. Could it be because they're insecure or they feel judged by you when you're not acting like them? Don't assume anything. Just come up with some ideas about what's going on for them and why they're acting this way.

Before the next time you hang out, have a script prepared so you'll feel confident about whatever it is you want to say. Using the both/and technique, find a way to express that you understand why they want you to do what they're doing. In other words, instead of criticizing their choices, acknowledge that they're having fun in the ways they choose to. Say, "It does sound like fun," if that's true for you.

What to Say

The purpose of the both/and technique is to acknowledge that you can be right and they can be right at the same time. Remember, nobody's completely wrong here—even the wildest ideas have a little bit of truth behind them, depending on the person. You may feel that smoking cigarettes is bad for your health, your friends may say it reduces stress and "isn't the worst thing." In this case, there is truth to both sides of the story. So don't criticize them; and just as importantly, don't apologize for your own choices. Saying "I'm sorry" or "please don't get mad at me" only reinforces the false idea that you're doing something wrong, and it takes away from what you're actually doing, which is asserting yourself.

Here are some ideas for your script. Pick one statement from each section to form a response that works best for you in your situation—any combination of them will work. Example: (Empathize) "I can see why you'd think I'm a party pooper." (And/Both Statement) "And I have so much to do; I really can't!" (Moving-On Statement) "Call me later, and let me know what happened."

Empathize (pick one)

* "That does sound like a lot of fun."

* "I understand why you'd want me to join in."

* "I can see why you'd think I'm a party pooper."

* "Thanks for thinking of me."

* "I know. I wish I could hang out more."

* "It probably seems like I'm always bailing."

Both/And Statement (pick one)

Use a both/and statement ("and," "and at the same time," "and you know me") plus one of the following reasons. Or try the statements below without "and" if that feels more comfortable for you.

* "I have so much to do; I really can't."

* "I'm not in the mood."

* "I'm just not up for it."

* "My parents are on my back about everything these days."

* "It's not my thing."

* "I've got way too much work right now."

Moving-On Statement (pick one)

* "Let's hang out later this week. When are you guys free?"

* "Have fun, and text me later, okay?"

* "Don't have too much fun without me!"

* "Let's do _____ (sober/legal activity) later this week."

* "Call me later, and let me know what happened!"

* "Want to do something this weekend?"

What to Do When...

What if you're worried that your friends are doing something dangerous? Any good friend would be concerned if she sees her friends making bad decisions or engaging in risky behavior. But what are you supposed to do? Having a conversation with them about it is probably about as appealing as getting a cavity filled. Use the tools from the previous section to be supportive, not blaming or attacking. It's best to address one topic at a time, rather than the whole host of risky behaviors at once. Here's an example:

> *It seems like you guys are having a lot of fun. You know me—I'm a worrier, and I am so scared you could get caught if you leave campus to smoke. Your parents would freak out! Do what you want. I'm here, though, if you ever feel like staying on campus instead.*

Notice how the last sentence was supportive and not judgmental. Ending your statement this way will help you with your goal of maintaining the friendship. You can't force others to make the same decisions as you, but can live your own truth and be there if and when they change their mind.

Write Your Script: Now try making your own. It can be used for peer pressure, problems with parents, or any communication mishap where you have to find a little truth to keep an argument from forming.

Reflection Questions: How would you use the both/and technique with the peer pressure you face in your own life?

What would you do if your friends were involved with dangerous behaviors like drugs, unprotected sex, or drinking and driving? Would you say something? If so, what would you say, and to whom would you say it?

Been There, Done That—Advice from Women Who've Been in Your Shoes

Haley Kilpatrick is an author, speaker, and founder and executive director of the national nonprofit organization Girl Talk, and the author of *The Drama Years: Real Girls Talk About Surviving Middle School—Bullies, Brands, Body Image, and More.* Haley understood the pressure to fit in, but instead stayed true to her values and found friends to support her.

Friday night football games were the worst! After the game, it was heartbreaking to see "my friends" pile into a Suburban for a not so discreet sleepover. Yet, sometimes they'd be nice to me, and I'd think we were friends. The constant back and forth was overwhelming and exhausting. School quickly became a place I dreaded. My grades began to drop because I couldn't focus in class. I was never sure when I was going to be given that look, when I would be worrying what was going to happen in the cafeteria, or why the girls around me were passing notes.

I met Christie, a high school friend through my school dance team. Since she was four years older (and captain of our dance team), she shared that she'd had a really hard time too, but she'd gotten through it, and she was certain that I would. "Forget about them," she'd say. "Let's go to the mall." I remember thinking to myself: if she thinks I'm cool enough to hang out with, I can't be that bad. Christie inspired me to keep going with my head held high.

When I was in my sophomore year of high school I decided to create a solution. It doesn't have to be this way, I thought. I started Girl Talk in 2002, a peer-to-peer mentoring program when I was fifteen, and we've grown to reach more than 40,000 girls. Instead of staying silent, I created a solution.

The Situation: Apparently, I'm Having a Party

My mom just changed her work schedule and now doesn't get home until 8 p.m. This is awesome because I don't have to be bothered by her when I get home, and I get so much more freedom—finally! I told some of my friends, and now they're planning a "get together" at my house but they didn't even ask me! Everyone is planning on showing up tomorrow, including my crush, and I know someone is going to bring alcohol or pot. I don't know how to cancel without looking like a loser.

It's frustrating when your friends are making decisions on your behalf. And of course it's a lot harder to say no when the situation involves someone you want to impress (your crush), plus the chance to be the girl with the "cool" house. What you need to do is look at all the what-ifs—not just the good things that could come from it. Take an honest look at all the possible outcomes if you give in to the peer pressure. (Even if you can't relate to the pressure to have a party, it's likely you'll at some point experience friends trying to push you to do something that doesn't feel right to you. So it's worth thinking about how to handle situations like this.)

Before You Say a Word

Go back and look at the list of rights presented earlier in this chapter. "You have the right to put your own needs ahead of your peers" is the one that needs to be in the forefront of your mind. Your "friends" are looking for a place to party, and it just so happens you have a supervision-free zone at their service. Their desire to party doesn't take precedence over your right to decide whether you want to offer your house for that purpose.

Let's evaluate the what-ifs:

* If your mom found out, would it be back to a babysitter and loss of your newfound freedom?

* If you cancelled the plan, would your friends be mad at you for eternity or would they get over it eventually? (And if they didn't respect your reasons, what would that say about them?)

* Would your crush respect you more or less if you stood up for yourself and set your own boundaries? (And if he or she didn't, what would that say about him or her?)

* Would you have a good time if you let the party happen, or would you be too anxious or worried to even enjoy yourself?

* What if alcohol or drugs were involved and an accident or medical emergency occurred?

In considering all the what-ifs, keep in mind that outcomes can be impossible to predict but are important to think about. Here are some stories from girls in similar situations who gave in to the pressure to host a party without permission:

My neighbors came over to check on me when my parents were at a late dinner party. (The neighbors have a spare key.) They walked in on my party and found me making out on the couch! Needless to say, I was mortified, and my parents totally found out. Emily, 16

My friend posted a picture of herself at my house with a beer bottle in the background, along with our kitchen's backsplash. My parents saw it, and I got grounded for a month. So not worth it. Sara, 14

I thought I cleaned everything up after a party in my basement. I didn't think to look in the bathroom, where someone had thrown away a beer bottle. My dad found it, and I had no alibi. Ali, 17

I had a few people over after school and didn't tell my parents. One of my friends forgot to take her medication and wound up having a seizure. I had to call my mom for help and obviously got caught. Maya, 16

The point of these stories is that even if you think about what's *likely* to happen, there are many other things that *could* happen. Use that to your advantage if you need to explain why you're saying no.

Set the Scene

It sounds as if your friends are really not looking out for you. So if you're not comfortable with the plan, it's up to you to assert yourself and say no. In this scenario, you're in luck because most of the communication has been via text. So it should be easy enough to tell everyone the party's off. You have more than one fire to put out, though. The second one requires a face-to-face convo with the friends who put you in this predicament.

What to Say

It may be easier to let your friends down if you also let them know what's at stake for you. Mention some of the what-ifs that apply to this situation: "My mom will probably ask the neighbors to check on me. She might get off early—I can't risk it." Let them know that you value your newfound freedom over one afternoon of your life.

You might want to say you're sorry, if you let them think the get-together was a go or if you feel bad about leaving them without a place to party, but don't over-apologize. Here are a few options, depending on your comfort level:

* If you're feeling brave, tell it to them straight. Text your crew: "Sorry guys, tomorrow's off. Can't have a party while my mom's at work." Or simply, "Party at my place is cancelled. Sorry."

* If you feel nervous about upsetting them, take a what-if statement and make it appear like more of a reality: "No party tomorrow. My mom may be getting off work early." Or "The party's off, my mom's schedule is changing." Or "Mom's got my neighbors on the lookout, the party's a no-go."

* It's better not to be wishy-washy (as in "It's not looking good" or "Maybe another time"). You don't want them to think you're not sure of yourself, and you don't want to find yourself in the same situation later.

The next step is talking to the friends who planned a party at your place without your permission. The best way to make sure they hear you is by talking in person. Use the sandwich technique from chapter 2 to express to them why it wasn't cool and what you want them to do differently next time (be brief):

Bread (positive statement): "I know it would be fun to hang out."

Peanut butter (assertive statement): "It's really not okay to plan a party at my house without talking to me about it first. Next time you have an idea like that, will you talk to me before inviting other people?"

Bread (empathic statement): "I'm sure you weren't trying to be disrespectful."

Director's Note

Don't let others pressure you.
When you give in to others, you
give away your self-respect.

#ExpressYourself

What to Do When...

What if they persist and try to talk you into it? "It will just be a few of us. She'll never find out." "That's so lame. Now we have nowhere to go." These examples of spoken peer pressure show you that your friends' agenda is much more important to them than the consequences you may face.

You can also use the both/and technique from earlier in this chapter to show them you're not going to be a pushover: "I wish I could help, and at the same time I am not going to risk my newfound freedom." If they don't respect what you're saying, leave it at that. There's no need to apologize for your right to say no.

> **Reflection Questions:** What would you say to your friends if they made a risky decision on your behalf that involved you or your property?
>
> Do you have any friends who do this or would do this to you? Would you find it hard to say no to those friends? What would you be afraid of?

The Situation: Quick Fix or Prescription for Problems?

Around midterms, a lot of people shell out their allowance for "study drugs," sold to them by other students. I've always thought that it's stupid to take a medication that isn't mine— dangerous, really. Until this year. Now I'm overwhelmed with midterms and my SAT class, and I'm having a hard time studying because I'm so tired all the time. All my friends are studying in the library, breezing through their books because they're all taking this study drug. I feel like if I want to make the grade, I've got to take it too.

This is an example of a serious form of unspoken pressure. Though no one is trying to talk you into taking this drug, it seems as if everyone's doing it, and you see it working for them. Your initial hesitation to take something you know is dangerous—deadly, even—should be a sign that it's probably not a good idea. You do need to weigh the pros and cons, but first you have to tune in to to what your intuition is telling you because your intuition is usually right about these things.

Before You Say a Word

Let's get real for a moment. No matter what drug it is, a prescription that belongs to someone else doesn't belong in your mouth or in your backpack. The reality is, if you get caught, you could end up expelled, in jail, or in juvenile hall. More importantly, if it's not meant for you, it could even be deadly. Consider these facts:

* The Drug Enforcement Administration lists prescription stimulants such as Adderall, Vyvanse, Ritalin, and Focalin as class 2 controlled substances—the same as cocaine and morphine. That means they carry high legal risks. Giving away your prescription, buying some pills from a friend, or having some in your purse without a prescription can be prosecuted as a felony—which means jail.

* No matter what the prescription, the side effects could really hurt you, or even kill you. If a doctor hasn't prescribed the medication specifically for you, you (or your best friend or your drug dealer) won't be able to predict how your body will respond. Possible effects include uncontrollable tics, muscle spasms, slurred speech, blurred vision, nausea, sweating, heart palpitations, and even heart attack.

139

You can use the pros and cons exercise from chapter 4 to help you make a decision. Take out a piece of paper and make a chart that looks something like this:

Pros of Taking It

* I would be more focused.
* I could get everything done.
* I might get better grades.
* It's exciting.

Cons of Taking It

* My parents or teachers might be able to tell that I'm on it.
* I could get in trouble.
* It may have bad side effects.
* I may lose some self-respect.

Pros of Not Taking It

* I won't have to worry about consequences.
* I won't lose self-respect.

Cons of Not Taking It

* I won't feel better about my workload.
* It'll be harder to get all my work done.
* My grades might not be as good.

(Notice the words "could" and "might." You can never be sure of the outcome, and possibility is not the same as likelihood. If you *might* get better grades, that doesn't mean you will.)

Look back over your chart and identify which of these feelings and consequences are short-term (lasting no longer than a day or two) and which are long-term (meaning they could last weeks, months, or years). Carefully consider all the possible consequences, especially the ones that could stick with you for the long term. Then decide whether it's worth it.

Set the Scene

Talk to one of your most supportive friends and let her know that you are resisting the temptation to take this drug. Ask her to help keep you accountable.

There are at least three people you may want to talk to about this situation: yourself, your accountability buddy, and the drug dealer. (Yes, that fourteen-year-old girl in your algebra class who's offering her Adderall is a drug dealer. Whether she's giving it away or selling it, if she's caught, she'll be considered a criminal.)

What to Say

* To yourself: This is where you might need to try that actor's warm-up exercise again. Tune in and listen to your intuition, your inner guide, or your gut. What is it telling you to do? Ask yourself whether you want to risk your future for a quick fix that could be harmful to your health or get you in a lot of trouble.

* To your friend: Ask your friend if she's faced a similar temptation, and if so, how she handled it (or if not, how she would). Ask if you can call on her for support when you're feeling the urge to give in. Maybe you can offer the same for her.

* To the drug dealer: Review the simple ways to say no from earlier in this chapter and come up with some new ones that fit this situation. For example:

  * "No. Thanks for asking, though."

  * "Nah, it wouldn't be good for me."

  * "No thanks. I don't need it."

What to Do When...

What if it's not a prescription but something "natural" and not a study drug but one that your friends are using to have fun? Whether it's pot brownies or "Molly" (MDMA, or ecstasy), the concerns are still the same. You never know how any drug or medication will affect you. Even if marijuana is legal in some states, it's not legal for you unless you have a prescription. The amount of THC (the main mind-altering ingredient) in marijuana varies; and unless you harvested it yourself, you don't know how many hands have touched it or what other substances may be in it. "Bad trips" or freak-outs often occur because of other chemicals added into the pot.

Many high school students think Molly is "pure." But in fact MDMA is a chemical that has been reported to cause intense, prolonged panic attacks, depression, psychosis, seizures, and even death. Get caught with this drug on you, and you may as well say peace-out to your friends—you may be expelled, placed in an intensive therapy program, or even sent to a treatment center if your parents or school find out.

As we've shown in this chapter, there are high stakes when it comes to peer pressure. Speaking up for what's in your best interest (or the interest of others) becomes even more important when the consequences of not doing so are potentially dangerous. Remember, you're the one in the director's chair, and you hold primary responsibility for your movie. You'll want to take into consideration the opinions of your cast and crew, but it's up to you to make the ultimate decisions and create a movie you can be proud of.

The next chapter continues the discussion of how to deal with pressure, but this time focused on romantic and sexual relationships. It will address situations in which you might feel pressured to do things you don't feel ready for. You will learn how to confidently express yourself in your relationships, without losing your heart, your mind, or your self-respect.

Director's Note

Your future depends on the decisions you make today.
Don't look back with regret.

#ExpressYourself

Chapter 6

Romantic Relationships

*When someone shows you how little you mean to them
and you keep coming back for more, before you know it,
you start to mean less to yourself.*

— Lena Dunham, *Not That Kind of Girl*

Have you ever felt super embarassed after a run-in with a crush—talked too much or said something so awkward that you're *still* blushing about it? Maybe you've felt pressure to hook up with someone you're not really into because everyone else *seems* to be doing it? Have you ever been disrespected by a partner or even wanted to break up but didn't know what to say or do? If so, then this chapter is for you. Romance is tricky for people of any age, but when you learn how to express yourself, you're more likely to feel and appear more confident—which is the most attractive attribute ever.

Let's start, once again, in the director's chair. In the movie of your life, who do you want on your set? As the director, you get to decide. That might seem easy, but it can be hard when you're attracted to or extra emotional about a certain cast member.

You may have a good idea of what, or *who*, is a good fit for you and your "movie" but if you aren't careful, you may allow some sucky people onto the set, which will mess with your movie big time. Unfortunately, in the world of romance, even the director can get blinded by special effects—or a special someone. That hottie in your English class can charm the pants off you—literally—so you'll need to find a way to keep your cool if you're not comfortable with his advances. If you let your emotions take over, you're more likely to veer too far from your script and may do things you'll later regret.

Crushes, romances, hookups, and breakups can be emotional roller coasters for anyone, not just teens. What makes this even more confusing is that your friends and family often chime in with their views on your love life. For instance, if your parents freak out over the idea of you dating, their advice will be tainted by their emotions. As a result, you're more likely to feel invalidated or upset. Friends may have a biased view, often due to jealousy and lack of experience in relationships—yes, even your friend who's had seven boyfriends isn't an expert. So how do you know what to do with their feedback? In order to make decisions about relationships, you've got to get clear on who you are and what you want, need, and deserve from that special someone.

In this book, the term "romantic partner" is used to refer to both males and females. Sexuality, especially for teenagers, can be fluid; some girls like girls, some like boys, and others like both. So instead of getting caught up in gender, simply apply the skills and scripts in this chapter to whatever situations you are in. Remember, these are just scripts—when you take them off the page, you have total creative freedom; you are the director.

Setting Boundaries

Along with a dose of confidence, healthy relationships require good communication skills. No matter what your relationship status is—single, casually hooking up, in a long-term relationship, or "it's complicated"—having a good idea of where you stand is key to setting and maintaining appropriate boundaries.

Boundaries are all about respect, and negotiating them is an important part of every relationship. Before you even say hello to someone you're romantically interested in, it's good to know where you yourself stand on personal space and how comfortable you are with different situations. Once you develop strong feelings for someone, it can be hard to act assertively, so it's better to have a solid sense of what you're cool with before locking lips. What is too far or too much for you? Use the exercise below to help you figure that out.

Director's Note

When you respect yourself, you show others
how to respect you.

#ExpressYourself

Exercise: Your Ideal Romantic Relationship

Answer the following questions, either in your journal or in your mind, to help you get clear on what you want from a romantic relationship. What qualities are "musts" in your ideal romantic partner? List all the personality traits, values, interests, after-school activities, and physical attributes you would like this person to have.

1. How do you want to feel when you are with this person?

2. How do you want this person to feel around you?

3. How will this person show that he or she respects you? And how will you show respect for him or her?

4. How much time do you want to spend together, and how much time apart?

5. How do you want to communicate with this person? Texting? Chatting? In person? In private? In groups?

Getting Physical

When it comes to physical contact, it's important to think ahead about how far you want to go so you don't end up crossing boundaries unintentionally. What you're comfortable with can change, of course, depending on the person and the situation, but it's helpful to have a general sense of what feels right versus what's going too far. Consider the following scenarios:

1. The crush you've had since middle school finally kisses you at a party. How far would you be comfortable going that night?

2. You've been casually dating or hooking up with someone, but the two of you haven't committed to being exclusive. What would you be comfortable doing sexually?

3. Your ex, whom you still have feelings for, wants to be "friends with benefits." How would you feel about that?

4. Your romantic interest wants to engage in sexting. What are you comfortable sharing online or via text?

Your responses to these questions should provide you with a little more insight on your sexual boundaries. It's natural for these boundaries to adjust over time, but pay careful attention to who wants the adjustments—you or your romantic partner? Allowing someone to bulldoze your boundaries is almost sure to cause regret and will likely end the relationship. Honoring your own boundaries shows confidence and self-respect and is much more likely to lead to the kind of relationship you want.

When it comes to romantic relationships, the right to set your own boundaries is the most fundamental right there is. But when you're feeling pressured or confused, it can be easy to forget that.

Your Rights

* You have the right to say no to anything that makes you feel uncomfortable.

* You have the right to your own personal space and alone time.

* You have the right to act according to your values.

* You have the right to express your wants and needs to your partner.

* You have the right to take things at your own pace.

* You have the right to be treated with respect.

* You have the right to refuse sexual advances, regardless of what you've done in the past.

* You have the right to end any relationship.

Which of these statements do you agree with? Are there some that you need to work on remembering? If so, which ones? Are there more rights that you would add to this list? Refer back to it whenever you find yourself questioning your own boundaries or trying to explain them to others.

Relationships are supposed to be fun and provide opportunities for emotional growth. But when emotions are running high, it can sometimes be hard to get along. When conflict comes up, you might not know what to say or do, especially if you haven't had much experience with relationships. The situations in this chapter will show you how to communicate in a cool and confident manner so you're more likely to be heard and understood by your special someone.

Director's Note

It is up to you to respect yourself & protect yourself.
Use your voice to protect you, not wreck you.

#ExpressYourself

The Situation: Is There a Label for This?

I just started seeing someone, and I don't want to scare him by talking about "labeling" the relationship. We talk every day and have fooled around, but I don't want to go too far without knowing whether we're a "couple" or not. I want to be exclusive, but I'm scared to tell him.

It's good for both individuals in a relationship to be on the same page. To have the healthiest relationship, each partner should know the other's desires, goals, fears, and limits. In the beginning of a budding romance, the fear of being rejected or freaking the other person out can keep you from saying what you want and need. Ironically, keeping those feelings and concerns inside is often what complicates or kills a possible love story. When you don't share what you're thinking, your partner will be more inclined to act passive-aggressively instead of supportively. Romantic partners can't read your mind—nobody can. Even when they sense that something's up, they may not know how to ask you about it. So the goal here is to speak up and respect yourself and your partner. That means that you've got to use the skills that help you say it right.

Set the Scene

Texting or talking online may seem like the easiest way to express yourself, but be warned, it can backfire. As you learned in chapter 4, relying on what you type can often lead to misunderstandings because it doesn't allow you to hear the tone of what is being said. Also, you have to sit with the anxiety of waiting for a response. Important topics deserve face-to-face conversation. So set the scene the next time you're hanging out.

Approach your conversation with a casual and confident tone. You may be nervous about all the what-ifs, but remember that "you can act" the part of a cool, confident, and self-respecting chick; and the more you play it, the more you'll feel confident and radiate it. (If it turns out he doesn't seem to care, then thank goodness you spoke up now before investing a lot more time and energy in this relationship.)

What to Say

Writing your script is often the hardest part. So here's where you might want to refer back to an acronym introduced in chapter 2: *HEARD*. Here's a brief review of what it stands for:

H: Have one sentence about the problem behavior ready. Ask yourself, *What's the intention here?* In this case, the answer is to identify whether you are exclusive or just hooking up. "I'm a little anxious about this—about me and you."

E: Express yourself. "I have so much fun hanging out with you, and I like where this is headed."

A: Ask for what you want or need. "Are we a thing? Are we seeing other people or are we exclusive?"

R: Reiterate what you want, and explain how it will help both of you. "I'd feel less anxious if I knew how you felt about this."

D: Don't get sidetracked. You're not asking him to dictate the terms of your relationship; you're simply asking where he stands at the moment to see if you are on the same page. You're not being needy; you're being inquisitive. In order for you to feel respected, you have to know where both of you stand. So in this situation, as in any situation, don't apologize for asking for what you deserve.

What to Do When

Of course you hope that your crush will turn into a dream boyfriend or girlfriend. But here comes the plot twist: What happens if he says he's not into a serious relationship right now and just wants to keep it "casual"? It may feel like you just got punched in the stomach. But keep in mind, the fact that he wasn't confident enough to bring it up and let you know where he stands means he's not as mature as you are. Before you rip into him, consider that there could be other things at play.

1. He is getting to know you, and it could just be too soon for him to feel committed to you. No need to give him an ultimatum right away, if you're willing to give it some time.

2. If he says he wants to keep it light and casual, that doesn't necessarily mean he's being disrespectful to you. It may just mean he's not ready for something more. So try not to get overly emotional or aggressive when communicating. Instead, get assertive. It is important for you to respect your boundaries and express yourself, which can totally be done without sounding demanding or desperate.

Here's one possible script. Pick the statements you like best in each section:

* Rephrase what you hear or think you hear.

   "It sounds like you aren't feeling as committed as I am."

   "It seems like you're more comfortable being casual than being exclusive."

* Acknowledge the truth in what he is saying to show you're not trying to start an argument.

   "It's normal to have different opinions on this; that's why I'm bringing it up."

   "You may be totally comfortable with just hooking up, and that's why I asked you."

* Say what you feel without criticism or sarcasm.

   "I've got to be honest and let you know that I just don't feel as comfortable hooking up."

   "I'm feeling uncomfortable; I'm just not cool with hooking up without being exclusive at this point."

* End with an idea or a question. Maybe suggest you both take some time to think about it. It's hard to make good decisions under pressure.

   "I think it's best that we take some time to think about whether we want to continue seeing each other."

   "It sounds like we both need to take some time to think about this; don't you think?"

* If, after your conversation, you're sure you want to end the relationship, say it in a matter-of-fact way, ideally with a little empathy.

   "It sounds like you're more comfortable with dating other people, which is your choice. That's not my style, so I think it's best that we move on."

The Situation: I'm So Confused!

Lots of my female friends like both boys and girls. I haven't had much experience in the romance department, and I thought I was into guys, but now I don't know. One of the pretty and popular girls in my school has become a close friend. She is super experienced with boys and girls, and I really want to be like her. She told me I needed to get more comfortable and said that the next time we hang out she will show me how. I really like her, but I don't know if I'm attracted to her. I am afraid if I say no, it will hurt our friendship. But if I say yes, what if I regret it? What do I do?

Many young people like to try on different hats when it comes to sexuality. That only becomes a problem if you feel pressured to do something that you're not comfortable with. In the last chapter we talked about spoken and unspoken peer pressure. Regardless of gender, feeling like you should hook up with someone because everyone else seems to be hooking up is an example of unspoken peer pressure. You're acting a certain way because you don't want to feel or be seen as different. What your friend is doing is an example of spoken pressure—telling you that you need more experience and pushing you rather than asking what you're comfortable with. Giving in to this pressure without first figuring out what you want can result in disaster.

Before You Say a Word

You may be really confused—that's normal. So before making a move, clarify your immediate goals. You want to keep your friendship with this girl, but you also don't know whether you want to be more than just friends. This is one of those times when you need to tune in to your gut feeling. It might be useful to do the exercise presented in chapter 5: Sit back for a minute and just focus on your breath. Inhale through your nose for five counts, then exhale through your mouth for five counts. Do this several times, and see if it helps you to get clear on what your gut is telling you to do.

Having a hard time still? Use the pros and cons exercise from chapter 4 to help you make a decision.

Pros of Hooking Up

* It will give me more experience.

* I might impress her.

* It seems exciting.

* _____

Cons of Hooking Up

* It could end up hurting my friendship.

* I might regret it.

* I might be the subject of gossip.

* _____

Pros of Not Hooking Up	Cons of Not Hooking Up
✱ I won't feel like I gave in to pressure.	✱ I won't be any more experienced.
✱ I won't complicate the friendship.	✱ My friend might be mad at me.
✱ _____	✱ _____

Set the Scene

As awkward as it may be to have a conversation with your friend, the sooner you have it, the better. It's like pulling off a Band-Aid—the quicker you do it, the less pain there will be. Plus, by being assertive, you won't have to spend any more time worrying about the situation.

What to Say

If you're feeling uneasy or hesitant, trust your intuition. It's your gut telling you that maybe this isn't a good idea, so don't do it. You don't want to complicate the friendship or regret hooking up. This is a perfect example of a situation where assertiveness will allow you to be respectful of your friend's feelings and your own. A gentle and direct approach means expressing your needs and maintaining the relationship. The sandwich technique is a good one to use in this situation.

Bread: Be gentle and positive. "That's really sweet of you."

Peanut butter: Assert what you need nicely. "I feel like it wouldn't be a good idea. It could make our friendship complicated or uncomfortable, which would be terrible."

Bread: Explain how this will benefit you and your friendship. "You're one of my closest friends, and I want to keep it that way."

Remember: Avoid "you" statements. And don't avoid the conversation or put it off. Imagine you were in her shoes; it would feel like you're being rejected, right? Expressing your feelings in words is almost always the most effective—and respectful—thing to do when trying to keep a friendship from getting complicated.

What to Do When

What if she gets offended? Or pushy? Remember, you are the director. It's not cool for anyone else to come on the set and try to take over your directing role. Although she may be more sexually experienced than you and really like you in a "more than a friend" way, you have to stick to what your gut tells you.

If your friend doesn't react well, use your listening skills to let her know that you're not intending to start an argument. Reflect her words or feelings. Paraphrase what you hear to let her know you heard her. She may respond by acting defensive or arguing with you, but over time reflecting will help her feel heard, and she will understand that there's little to argue with— you're just standing up for yourself. Here are some examples of reflecting statements:

* "It sounds like..."

* "It seems like you're feeling..."

* "I hear what you're saying, that I am..."

* "It feels like..."

Let's put this skill into practice in this situation.

She appears frustrated, embarrassed, or hurt, and says: "You know, I was just trying to help!"

You respond with empathy and caring: "It seems like you're upset with me. I wasn't trying to hurt your feelings, and I'm sorry if I did."

It can also help to ask more questions about what she's thinking and feeling: "What do you think we can do to make things cool between us again?" That will get her brain moving away from the problem and toward a solution.

Reflection Questions: If you were in this situation, do you think you and your friend would be able to stay "just friends" after this conversation? In a few days or weeks, would everything be back to normal? Why or why not?

If your friend pressured you like this, how would you feel about it, and how would you react?

The Situation: We Always Argue!

My boyfriend and I argue—a lot. He always takes forever to respond to my texts, is always busy with homework or friends, and never has time to spend with me. When I try and talk to him about it he says I'm being "whiny" or "needy." We have a lot of fun when we're alone, but he gets mad if I bother him when he's busy. That's just one of the many things we fight over. I don't like the way he's treating me, and I am sick and tired of arguing all the time. I want to make things better, but I don't know what to do.

It sounds like your boyfriend isn't hearing what you're trying to say. If you want him to understand what's bothering you, you may need to make your message clearer. You need to let him know that you want to feel important to him and that it hurts when he treats you like his girlfriend only when it's convenient. The trick is to make sure you're phrasing it in a way that helps him see that you are trying to improve the relationship. He may not be mature enough to take your feelings seriously or to respond honestly about his own feelings, but at least you will have done your part to start the conversation and stop the fighting.

Before You Say a Word

It seems like you want to stay in the relationship and your goal is to improve it. Think back to the arguments you've had with your boyfriend. Are they usually via text or in person? Even if you're trying hard not to be annoying, texting can come across that way, especially when he's busy with his friends and you keep sending messages because you aren't getting the answer you want. In person, you have to pay attention to timing and avoid bringing up these issues when you're feeling super emotional or when either of you is stressed. Once you find the right time, approach him with a calm and confident tone of voice. (No sarcasm!)

Set the Scene

If another argument happens before you have some one-on-one time, here's how to handle it in the moment: If you're with friends or in public, make sure you step away from others' view and out of earshot. It will only embarrass both of you if your friends have front-row seats to the show. And no matter when and where you have this conversation, do yourself a favor and stick to one problem behavior, rather than opening up the whole bag of things he does that make you mad. Throwing too much at him (or anyone) at once is overwhelming and will likely make it more difficult for him to hear you.

What to Say

Your goal, of course, is to be heard. But here's the twist: before you describe your own feelings, it helps to get his attention by acknowledging and validating the way he may be feeling. Put yourself in his shoes for a second and see if you can understand why he may be saying the things he's saying. Have there been times when you've been whiny or appeared jealous (even with a good reason)? You don't have to agree with him; just show that you get why he feels the way he does.

Here are some possible ways to validate his feelings:

* "You're right; I'm being _____," or "I can see why you feel that I'm being _____." (Insert the character trait he is alluding to.)

* "It sounds like I really _____. That was not my intention, and I am sorry."

Once you've acknowledged his feelings, the next step is expressing your own feelings and desires:

* "It upsets me when we argue."

* "I would like to spend more time with you."

* "I'd like it if we could talk things out."

Ask him what he thinks:

* "Is this something you think we can try?"

* "What ideas do you have about how we can communicate better?"

What to Do When

Let's say he gets even more irritated and frustrated—not what you were going for. If you kept your cool and he flew off the handle, he is showing you he is not as mature as you. If you give in to childish behavior, you'll only reinforce it, and it will be more likely to continue. (It's like training a puppy; if you give him a treat after she has peed on the rug, you are telling him to keep doing it. Don't reinforce the bad behavior!) But don't ignore it, either. Instead, hold your head high and say, "I'll talk to you when you've calmed down." (It's like putting the puppy back in her crate and saying "no treat and no attention for you.") Hold on to your pride and your power by talking to people only when they are calm and, hopefully, respectful.

Reflection Questions: During an argument or disagreement with someone, how do you keep your cool? Do you ever feel the urge to yell, scream, or roll your eyes but resist it? How do you keep your anger from interfering with the argument?

How would you use (or rewrite) these scripts to address a conflict in your relationship?

The Situation: I'm Not Ready, But He Is

I have been dating my boyfriend for six months. This is my first real relationship. He has had several serious relationships, all of which involved sex. He knows I am a virgin and used to love that about me. Lately, I feel like he has been pressuring me to go all the way. He says things like "I think it's time," "I did with all my other girlfriends," and "I feel like if you really cared about us, then we would have already had sex." He has tried to have sex with me a few times, even though each time I said no and got upset, and he said he wouldn't do it again. I do really care about him and want to have sex with him eventually, but I just don't feel ready yet. I'm afraid he'll break up with me if I don't give in soon. How do I get our relationship back to the way it was?

Sexual activity in a relationship should be fun and feel safe, not forced. You don't owe anyone anything, especially not your body. Just because he's waited and wants it doesn't mean you have to do what he wants you to do. It doesn't matter if he buys you dinner, takes you to the concert of your dreams, or begs—your body isn't something he's getting until you've decided you want to give it. It isn't fair for your partner to claim that you don't care about him because you won't have sex. And you shouldn't feel guilty for not going all the way.

When your partner doesn't respect your sexual boundaries, there's a real danger that his (or her) behavior can cross over into sexual violence or abuse (see the list of signs below).

Before You Say a Word

The trickiest part of being in a romantic relationship is the confusion that can occur between what your mind tells you and what your gut tells you. You may be thinking, *He loves and respects me; he just gets caught up in the heat of the moment. He doesn't mean to pressure me.* Ask yourself, what you would tell a friend to do in this situation? Would you remind her how important it is to respect herself?

Look back at the "Your Rights" section earlier in this chapter and think about which ones are important to you. Ask yourself if some of these rights are not being respected, and if that's the case, is this the right guy for you? If you feel like trying to make it work, give yourself an ultimatum:

If he does _____, _____,
or _____, *I will end things.*

Even when you're not comfortable expressing your needs to your partner, you need to at least express them to yourself.

Set the Scene

Conversations about sensitive topics really need to happen face-to-face, not only because they can get emotional but also because you need to ensure that you're really heard and understood. And when you communicate by texting or messaging, you can't be sure the conversation will stay private.

What to Say

In order to be effective, you need to pick a tool that doesn't blame but explains. Your best bet is the *ASSERT* skill. Your goal, of course, is to be respected and to improve your relationship. But in addition to describing your own feelings, it helps to acknowledge or validate the way he may be feeling. Use empathy to come up with a statement that will resonate with him.

- **A:** Ask if he has a few minutes to talk. Even if you're hanging out alone, make sure that he is not distracted.

- **S:** Sound confident, not aggressive. Your tone of voice should reflect that you are respecting yourself. Avoid baby talk or speaking too softly.

- **S:** Describe the situation (briefly). "I'm feeling pressured to have sex."

- **E:** Express your feelings and empathize. "I know it may have been different with other girls—I'm a different person. I don't feel ready, and it makes me uncomfortable when you don't seem to respect that."

- **R:** Request what you want or need. "I really need you to slow down. Can you do that?"

- **T:** Tell him how making the change you want will help your relationship. "I know it can be difficult, but I think it will really make things more comfortable if we try taking it slow. Don't you?"

Don't allow the conversation to get sidetracked by his emotions or more pressure. Stick to what you want, which is no more verbal or physical pressure to have sex.

You can also try the sandwich technique, adding in some "jelly" to sweeten the conversation. The assertive statement is the sticky part (the peanut butter), which needs to be sandwiched between two positive statements (the bread) that will encourage him to listen and engage in the conversation. Here are some examples:

Bread (positive statement about relationship):

"You mean so much to me."

"I really love hanging out with you."

Peanut butter (assertive statement):

"I'm feeling pressure to have sex, and I'm not comfortable with it yet."

"I don't like to be pushed to do things I'm not ready for."

Jelly (some sweetness or empathy):

"I know other girls you've been with have been okay with it, so I'm sure it's difficult for you to slow down."

"I know you don't mean to pressure me; that's why I'm bringing it up."

Bread (reiterate positive):

"Can we just take it slow, and I'll let you know when I'm ready?"

"Do you think we can try taking it slow? It would make me feel so much better."

What to Do When

What if the pressure continues or gets worse? Assertiveness isn't always what you say, it's also what you do, such as leaving the situation or ending a relationship. You might start by leaving the situation; go home; go to a friend's; get out of the turmoil. You both are emotionally charged, and it's likely going to be hard to communicate. If your partner is doing any of the following, he may be crossing the line into abuse:

* Making you feel guilty or immature when you don't consent to sexual activity.

* Physically forcing himself on you when you're not ready.

* Making fun of you or calling you names when you don't give in to what he wants.

Take these behaviors as cues to speak up more forcefully for what you want and deserve. Let him know the consequences (not in a threatening way) of disrespecting you:

* "I need you to please stop pushing me. I don't like it when you try to have sex with me, and it makes me very uncomfortable."

* "I'm not going to have sex with you anytime soon. If that's a problem, then we need to talk about the future."

The bottom line is that if he is unwilling to respect you now, he will be unlikely to respect you in other situations as well. The assertive director puts "me" before "we." If you are feeling as though things need to cool off or end because you are not being respected, the next situation may help. So think about whether a relationship without mutual respect is a relationship you really want to continue.

The Situation: Facing My Ex for the First Time

My girlfriend just broke up with me, and I'm a mess. What makes it worse is that we go to the same school and have many of the same friends. I'm so angry and hurt, but I don't want to lose it at school. How do I keep it together when I face her for the first time?

Breaking up sucks. There is no other way to put it. Emotions are all over the place—you may feel like kicking your ex in the face and hugging her at the same time. The worst part about romance in high school is that if you attend the same school as your ex or have mutual friends, you're bound to run into your ex before you're ready. But this run-in doesn't have to be painful or awkward. The key is—you guessed it—assertiveness.

Before You Say a Word

There are a few things to do behind the scenes before bravely taking a step out of your tear-soaked pj's and arriving on set as a newly single girl. Although you may be feeling damaged and insecure, you're not playing that character today. Instead, you're showing confidence and respect, even if that means cracking a smile to the person who made you cry.

Ask yourself what image you want to give off—how would a confident character in your movie act? How would she treat herself, the people around her, and even the character who broke her heart? Would she fly off the handle and throw a punch or a bunch of cuss words across the hall? Or would she keep her composure and show the world her best self?

If your brain feels like it's been hijacked by the heartache, you may have forgotten some of your directing skills. Have no fear—this is just temporary. If it doesn't come naturally, remember, you can act the part. Envision the character you want to play. How would your character walk, talk, and feel? Confident? Strong? Friendly? Happy? What would she be wearing? Play your part. The scene won't last forever. You can run to the bathroom or your car or the arms of a friend, but try to wait until you've yelled "Cut!"

Set the Scene

Here are the dos and don'ts for a flawless performance:

* Don't come to school with mascara running down your face. The whole school doesn't need to see your pain.

* Don't post to social media all about it. (In fact, maybe avoid social media for a few days. Have a friend hide your ex from your accounts, and delete her number in your phone.)

* Don't be dramatic. Don't be the girl who tries to get back at her ex by obnoxiously flirting with people or who acts like she never existed. Both of those ways of acting just look forced and fake.

* Do show respect in the face of disrespect. If you pass her in the hall, see if you can manage a smile. Think about how you want to be treated, and treat her that way.

* Do your thing! Stick to all your normal routines. Eat lunch at the same table; take the same route in the halls. Don't let fear of a run-in keep you from living your life, and don't let your ex push you off your own set.

What to Say

Actions can speak louder than words, so you don't need to say too much, especially in your first run-in with your ex. If you're waiting for a good time to tell her how much she has ruined your life, this isn't it. Wait until you've chilled out and are not in public.

Smile. Research shows that when you smile, you actually stimulate areas of your brain that make you happy. And pay attention to your posture. Good posture shows confidence—without having to say a word! Bring your shoulders back, keep your head held high, and look straight ahead—not at your phone.

Scene: Between Classes

Whether you are at your locker with your crew or simply walking to class, this is a scene every high school student can relate to—the slow motion approach of someone you either really want to see or really want to avoid. Don't be afraid to make eye contact. A simple smile is ideal—not a flash of all your pearly whites, just an acknowledgment of her existence.

Scene: The Awkward Approach

If you are approached by your ex, don't freak out. Simply be polite. Make small talk; don't be dramatic or open up a can of worms. If she says, "Hey, how are you?" your line is "Good, how are you?" not "How am I? How do you think I am? I can't believe you have the nerve to ask me that!" Even if you feel like turning your back on her, stay in character and show respect for both her and yourself.

The Scene: Let's Talk

If she asks you to talk, and you're okay with it, try to make the conversation happen when you don't have a class to go to, a test to study for, or anything important right afterward. No matter what she says, even if it's sweet and apologetic, it will bring up emotions that will linger in your head all day long.

Here's a "breezy and busy" but still respectful response: "I can't right now; I've got so much to do. Let's talk later. Let me know when you're free." Your tone should be friendly and casual, emphasizing that you're not blowing her off, just putting yourself first.

If you choose to talk later, remember: If she can hurt you once, she can hurt you again. So be prepared. Set some boundaries, maybe a time limit. Have a friend wait in the car for you so you'll have a reason to cut the conversation short or someone to comfort you afterward.

What to Do When...

What if, instead of approaching you, she ignores you? That kind of behavior can be extremely upsetting. It also shows immaturity, and it's a good reminder of the possibility that your breakup was a blessing in disguise. The best way to handle it is to continue to treat her as you would anyone else—with a smile and a casual "hey." (You're the director—don't let her dictate the roles.) It may take a while to find out whether you two will be able to be friends. So for now, just give your emotions (and hers) some time to settle down.

The situations in the past two chapters addressed how to deal with some of the members of your cast and crew—your peers and your romantic partners. We've shown how, even when you're disrespected, you can still show respect and maintain your dignity. The next chapter will discuss other cast and crew members who may play equally important roles behind the scenes and have a huge impact on the final product: those are the adults in your life. Knowing how to interact with—and get what you want from—teachers, coaches, family friends, and employers or prospective employers will keep things running smoothly on set, even when the production doesn't go according to plan.

Director's Note

Don't put up with less than you're worth.

#ExpressYourself

Chapter 7

Powerful Adults & Professionals

If you're scared to step in to the big dreams that you have for yourself, just know that the universe is WAITING for you. We can't wait to see you shine and blossom, and we are in need of your truth. Even those things that you think there is no way you could ever do, you can and you were meant to.

— Nitika Chopra, Talk Show Host and Entrepreneur,
http://www.yourbellalife.com

By now, you probably have a pretty good sense of how to ask for what you want and need. But doing that with your friends or your parents is one thing; approaching other adults can be much more awkward. And when it's uncomfortable, you'll be tempted to avoid it altogether. Instead of asserting yourself— asking your teacher for an extension on your paper or making a pitch to your coach for more playing time—you'll have the urge to walk away.

But the thing is, you need these people to make your movie. Think the director just walks onto the set and yells, "Action!"? Not exactly. A big part of the project is learning from the experts, which requires asking for help and listening to their experience.

Isabella Rose Taylor is a thirteen-year-old fashion designer. Yes, that's right. Even before she was a teenager, the tween from Austin, Texas, was designing clothes and sewing up a storm, getting her first big break from none other than Nordstrom. How did someone so young manage to do something that few adults can even imagine? By believing in herself and not giving up, but also by asking for help. She may have had very little experience in the adult world, but she made the most of it. Getting her designs off the drawing boards and onto the runway took lots of communication with adults in her life and asking for help from many more besides her parents. She may have been intimidated by some of those adults, but she recognized that she needed them to help turn her dream into reality. In an interview with TODAY, Taylor said the key to her success has been blood, sweat, and glitter: "Blood, because it takes a lot of passion and sacrifice. Sweat, because of the time and hard work you must do. And glitter, because of the imagination and creativity. There must be a dream behind your business." But equally important is her willingness and ability to work with adults, because without their help, her business would be next to impossible.

You may not be interested in starting your own clothing line, but there are undoubtedly other reasons why you need to be comfortable talking to adults. An upcoming college visit, a job interview, a tutoring session, a doctor's appointment, a piano lesson—whatever the situation, this chapter will help you overcome your fears, and give you the tools to talk to adults with confidence to help you turn your dreams into reality.

The Intimidation Factor

Remember how your parents used to set up your sleepovers, e-mail your teachers with questions, and deal with all those uncomfortable adult conversations for you? As you get older, the adults in your life begin to expect to hear from *you*. In all honesty, most teachers, coaches, and employers don't want to talk to your parents—they want to talk to you. And your parents are probably ready to shift some responsibility over to you as well. Your mom may still make your dentist appointments or call the school when you're sick, but she's not going to call your boss to ask if you can change your shifts this week, right? Learning to accept these responsibilities is part of transitioning from little girl to independent woman.

Throughout your childhood, and even now, the adults in your life have been in a position of power. Now that you're close to adulthood yourself, it's time to start viewing them less in terms of power and more as your soon-to-be peers. You still need to treat adults with respect, but think of these relationships as more reciprocal. You provide them with many benefits, too. Many adults appreciate the things they learn from girls your age and value your experience and insight.

Director's Note

Intimidation is insecurity. Everyone is human; treat them that way.

#ExpressYourself

Exercise: Inventory of Important Adults

A little later we will talk about the importance of having a mentor, someone you look up to and who wants to help you achieve your dreams. But first things first: there are probably many adults already in your life who can help you in all sorts of ways. If you want to take advantage of that help, the best thing you can do is to set aside any negative judgments you have about these adults and get into a grateful state of mind. Gratitude has a way of turning your mind around and changing your attitude for the better. You don't have to pretend you like someone if you don't. You can say to yourself, for example, "Even though Ms. _____ is annoying and sometimes makes my life miserable, I am grateful that she..." This exercise will help you get into the right frame of mind and give you a chance to practice gratitude.

1. Think of a few adults in your life who have helped you recently. Who are they? What are you grateful for? Spend a few minutes writing about why you are grateful for whomever comes to mind.

2. Are there some adults in your life who you wish would just leave you alone? Can you think of something that you've learned from them or something else about them that you're grateful for?

3. Name some adults who are helping you achieve your academic goals or who would give you this kind of help if you asked for it. Write about how they are helping you.

4. Who could be used as references for college applications, job interviews, scholarships, or awards? (These can be people from your school or job, or friends of the family.) How are they helping you?

5. Who pushes you (in a good way)? A good coach, trainer, or instructor will help your body or mind go further than you thought it could and inspire you toward higher goals. How do these people push you?

6. Who helps keep you healthy? Are there health care practitioners, coun-
    selors, or others in your life who guide you in taking care of yourself?
    How are they helpful to you?

7. Who puts money in your pocket—a paycheck or allowance? (Include
    people who have helped you find jobs.) How have they helped you
    financially?

8. Who's your cheerleader? Which adults in your life see your potential and
    support your dreams? How do they support you?

9. Who gives you access that you wouldn't otherwise have? (Your best
    friend's parents, who invite you along on vacations? Your boyfriend's
    parents, who let you hang out at their house even when he's studying
    for finals?) What do they give you access to?

Your Rights

It may feel like adults have more power than you; sometimes
they do, but you always have the right to express yourself and
feel heard—this is a basic human right. Here are some rights to
remember when communicating with adults.

*   You have the right to ask questions; there are no stu-
    pid questions.

*   You have the right to say no to requests that don't
    feel good.

*   You have the right to be treated with respect.

*   You have the right to follow your dreams.

* You have the right to be paid on time and to ask for more money.

* You have the right to be friends with adults.

* You have the right to change your mind.

* You have the right to ask for help.

Communication in the Adult World

You may be so used to sending texts or instant messages to get in touch with people in your life that going beyond 140 characters is out of your comfort zone. But voice mail and e-mail are essential tools when it comes to communicating with busy adults. With voice mail, the key is to be both brief and polite. Always leave your name, phone number, and some idea of the times you can be reached. If you want to ask for something, go ahead and ask! But make sure to acknowledge that you know that person is busy and you understand that he or she may not have the time.

E-mail is an important mode of communication in the adult world. But even adults can make major mistakes that turn communication into miscommunication. Here are some tips to help you stay on track from the start.

E-mail Etiquette

Whether you're writing to a teacher, coach, employer, or other adult, start with a tone that's polite and professional, even if you know the person well. Use proper greetings, paragraphs, bullets, closings, and other features that give your letter a professional look. Good grammar is important too. All of these elements show that you're serious, mature, and savvy. If your correspondent replies in a casual tone, it's fine for you to shift to a more casual voice as well, but it's better not to start off that way because it can be taken as a lack of courtesy or respect.

* Always include a subject line so the recipient will know what it's about and how necessary it may be to reply right away. Make it a quick line about what you want or need—for example, "Question about Assignment 4."

* Address the person properly: "Dear _____," or "Hi Mr. _____." In your subsequent responses, continue to use the person's name. Otherwise, it looks as if you're rushing or as if you're passing him in the hall with a nod instead of stopping to say hi.

* Start with a greeting. Even if you couldn't care less how your English teacher is doing, act as though you care. Why? Because it's polite, it sets a positive tone for the e-mail, and it engages the person. Here are some examples:

  * "I hope this e-mail finds you well."

  * "I hope you're having a good day."

  * "It was nice speaking with you the other day."

* Write your reason for making contact. Whether it's a question, a concern, or a compliment, make it quick.

Consider using bullet points if you have multiple questions. Examples:

* "I have a question about the homework and was wondering if you would be able to meet with me before or after school to discuss it." (Unless it's a short, straightforward question, it's better to talk in person rather than pose the question in an e-mail.)

* If it is a simple question with, most likely, a simple answer: "I have a question about the homework that I was hoping you could answer. If it's better to ask you in person, just let me know, and I'd be happy to come in. Here's my question:"

* Express gratitude. Even if you think he's the worst teacher on the planet, you're asking for something (and anyway, kindness is always appropriate). Thank him for his time or whatever he is doing for you.

    * "Thank you for your time."

    * "I appreciate your help."

    * "Thanks so much."

* Sign off with a positive note such as "Best wishes," "Take care," or "Sincerely."

* If the purpose of your communication is a complaint, talking on the phone or in person would likely be a better option. If you do use e-mail, don't use it to get everything off your chest. Stick to the facts.

* Don't use texting language in an e-mail, ever.

* Think about the impression given by your e-mail name. Is it something like hotchick2000 or harry stylesGF? If it looks immature or inappropriate, it may have an effect on whether your e-mail is taken seriously. Try your first name, middle name, or last name mixed with a number you'll remember.

Regardless of whether you're communicating via phone, voice mail, e-mail, or in person, remember that the most important thing to include is a sincere expression of thanks. It shows that you're mature and considerate, and it will go a long way toward people's willingness to help you. Think about it: how generous would you be to someone who doesn't acknowledge your generosity?

Talking to Teachers

If you've fallen asleep in class or failed a test, it's not the end of the world, and it's not your final chance to make a good impression on your teacher. Teachers can be intimidating, but most of them truly care about their students and want to see them succeed. What frustrates them are the students who don't seem to care and who don't speak up when they need help. After all, no one can read your mind.

The important thing to remember is that teachers, for the most part, do want you to ask for help. Jessica Lahey, a teacher who also writes about education, explained it to me like this: "Asking for help shows that a student cares about their education, and that goes a long way with teachers who are being asked to grade students based on not only their scores and their work, but also their investment in learning."

So if you want to make a good impression on your teacher, follow Lahey's advice: "Teachers look for kids who want to learn. It's hard to fake, so they are easy to spot. True enthusiasm, rather than brownnosing, is a gift."

And once again, don't forget to express appreciation any time your teacher gives you some extra time or extra help. "Never underestimate the power of a thank-you note, but really any thank-you is great," Lahey said. "Teachers tend to hear mostly complaints, so the thank-yous can really fuel a teacher's enthusiasm."

Teachers aren't just there to help you make the grade; they can also be your ally in tough situations. Talking to a responsible adult—whose job it is to handle these kinds of situations—is often the most effective way get help when social injustices come into your life. The following story shows how it can work.

A friend of mine was being bullied after school by older, more popular girls who would push her, throw things at her, and trip her. I couldn't stand up to them; they were too powerful, and honestly, I thought they would hurt me or her if I tried. So I told my favorite teacher about it when I went in to get some help before school. She thanked me for being brave enough to speak up and said she would handle it. That afternoon, she was "coincidentally" in the hallway. She caught them in the act, and they ended up in serious trouble. So they stopped bullying my friend. And even though I didn't directly stand up to the bullies, I feel like I stood up for someone who didn't have a voice. And it had an effect." —Ava, 15

Ava's decision to speak up about the bullying she had witnessed was brave and bold. She knew that saying nothing would make her feel worse but that saying something to the bullies was too risky for her. Fortunately, most teachers and other adults will view you with respect when you help out a fellow student. They know how serious bullying is, and they will likely see you as a confident and caring student—plus they will keep your name out of it. If all else fails, tell a parent and have him or her contact the school.

Director's Note

Speaking up for others is brave and bold.
Bullying is cowardly and cruel.

#ExpressYourself

The Situation: Can Teachers *Really* Help Me?

I'm totally bombing my chemistry class. I just don't get it. I study all the time, but nothing seems to sink in. To make matters worse, I've forgotten to turn in a few homework assignments. I'm sure my teacher thinks I just don't care. I know I should go talk to her, but what do I say? How do I get her to see that I'm really trying, and how do I ask for help?

While it may not always seem like it, teachers are actually there to help you. Even if you've messed up in a major way—or especially if you've messed up in a major way—you really have nothing to lose by talking to your teacher. It's likely that the only thing keeping you from showing up at her desk with a list of questions is your discomfort. Keep in mind that if you fail the class, it makes the teacher look bad too, so the truth is that it benefits both of you if you make the mature move and ask for help.

Before You Say a Word

What's your goal? To get some tutoring? Or to see if she'll still give you some credit if you turn in those missing homework assignments? Whatever the specific goal, make sure to start out by asking for help, not by asking her to make an exception for you.

Set the Scene

If you feel more comfortable expressing yourself in an e-mail, review the tips above. It would probably be better, though, for you to use e-mail just to set up a time to talk. It's almost always a good idea to talk face-to-face with your teacher, especially if you want her to have some empathy and to understand that you really do want to improve your performance in the class. Avoiding this conversation, or putting it off, will only make things worse.

What to Say

Be honest and admit the ways you've messed up. Remember, your teacher doesn't want to ruin your life; she's there to help. When you arrive, ask whether it's a good time to talk. That shows you realize she's busy and you value her time.

Here's a simple formula for expressing yourself in this situation. All you have to do is fill in the blanks.

I feel...

Example: "I feel terrible about how I'm doing in class..."

because...

Example: "...because I care about my grades and I'm really interested in science, but I'm just having a hard time understanding chemistry."

Can you...?

Example: "Can you help me figure out a way to get back on track?"

Don't forget to admit whatever part is your fault; it will help if your teacher sees honesty, rather than defensiveness: "I know it seems like I'm not trying, and it's true that I forgot to turn in those last few homework assignments. I'm so lost, and I feel really bad about not asking for your help sooner. Do you have any suggestions?"

Here's an example of a student's e-mail to her teacher when she was having anxiety around turning in her paper.

Dear Ms. Smith,

I hope you are having a good evening. I am e-mailing you to see if we can find a time to talk about my essay that was due last week, and about my grade. I know I'm failing, and I'm embarrassed about it. I haven't turned in my essay because

I'm not feeling confident about my writing. Every time I think it's done, I find a reason I need to start over. In the past I've had some anxiety around writing. Do you think you could meet with me this week? If you let me know a few good times that work with your schedule, I will make one of them work.

I really appreciate your help with this, and I look forward to meeting with you. Thank you for your time.

Sincerely,
Emily R.

What to Do When...

What if your teacher tells you it's too late? You get to decide whether to accept that or keep pushing. But either way, your effort won't have been a waste of time. Expressing yourself and asking for what you need are important. Even if this teacher can't (or won't) help you in the moment, she may be able to point you in the direction of someone who can; if she's unwilling to help in the end, at the very least you've shown her you cared enough to make an effort.

If you decide to continue with your quest for help, come up with a specific idea. For example, suppose she says, "I don't think there's anything you can do except take better notes and study harder for the exams." You could respond with, "Sometimes I learn better from watching others do the problems. Could I schedule a time to come in and have you show me how you do it?" The worst that could happen is that she'll say no, but at least she'll know you're serious about wanting to learn and do well in the class.

The Situation: My Coach Is Being Unfair!

I've been playing my heart out in soccer and have been in my position for years. Now all of a sudden my coach isn't starting me anymore, and a girl who isn't as good (no offense) is taking my spot. Even worse, he's putting me in positions I've never played before. I asked him what's up, and he said, "We're trying something new, and I need you to be a team player." I asked him again after practice last week if he thinks I will be able to start, and he said, "You need to start acting like a team player or else you're not going to play at all." I'm now starting to hate soccer, and it's all because of him.

Adults aren't always very savvy when it comes to talking to teenagers. They may think you're tougher than you really are. They may speak to you the way they were spoken to as a teen because that's what feels comfortable to them. Or they may just have poor communication skills in general. None of those things excuses them from listening to you and considering your needs, but you may need to think of your coach's shortcomings as roadblocks and to come up with a strategy to navigate around them so you can get where you want to go.

Before You Say a Word

When you come across an adult with a difficult personality, the best strategy is to stay focused on what you want. In this situation, you want your coach to put you in the game, in the position you want. How you communicate that is important. First, consider whether there's something in your attitude that might be sending your coach a different message. Have you been coming late to practice or disregarding your coach's instructions? Are there things you need to change to show that you really are a team player?

Then give some thought to your communication style. When talking to your coach and asking for what you want, are you being both assertive and respectful? Or are you whining or sulking? Once you've examined your own behavior, think about your coach, but with a more empathetic perspective. Is he super busy right now? Are there difficult circumstances he has to deal with? Maybe there's pressure from another coach or parent to make some changes? Or maybe he's just having a bad week? Adults have problems too. And their jobs may be much more complicated than you realize. Teachers and coaches, especially, have a lot of other people besides you to listen to and accommodate.

Keeping all of these things in mind, try again to ask for what you want. The worst that will happen is he'll shoot you down and you'll have to come up with plan B. And at least you'll know that you gave it your best shot.

Set the Scene

If your coach is preparing for practice, or in a hurry, it may be the wrong time to talk to him—not only because you need his full attention, but also because you might be perceived as not respecting his time. Try taking it one step at a time. Start with an e-mail (or text if you're on texting terms with him) and ask about a good time to chat: "Hi Coach. I was wondering if you have some time this week to talk. Let me know when is good for you. I can come to practice early or stay late if that works. Thanks!" Setting the scene this way will most likely make you feel more confident and make your coach feel respected. He'll then be more likely to listen to what you have to say.

What to Say

Here's another chance to use the skills that we discussed in chapter 3, about talking to your parents. Acknowledge what you've already been told, and admit to any fault on your part before diving into what you want. Avoid getting too emotional or aggressive. Stay focused on your goal, which is to get more playing time—or at least to better understand your coach's reasons for benching you.

Here's an example: "Thanks for making the time to talk to me. I am trying to be patient, as you suggested the last time I asked you about this. I'm trying to accept that I'm no longer starting, but I could really use your help in understanding why. Is there something I did? And is there something I could be doing to get back on the field or back in my position?"

Or try the sandwich technique.

The "bread" is the way you ease into the conversation: "Hey Coach, thanks for talking to me today."

The "peanut butter" is the content—the thoughts, feelings, or questions you want to communicate: "I'm confused about the recent change in my position. Can you help me understand the reasons why you made the change? I'd really like to start again." In order to be spreadable, the peanut butter should be smooth. That means your approach needs to include just one or two requests, not a flood of questions and feelings.

The "jelly" is how you "sweeten up" what you're saying, to make it easier to swallow. Empathy always works well: "I realize you're probably trying to give others more playing time." It's okay to spread the jelly before the peanut butter, if you think it will work better that way.

Once your coach has answered your questions, close your "sandwich" with another piece of bread: "Thanks for taking the time to explain your decisions to me."

What to Do When…

What if the coach says something rude or mean? This is something you may have been worried about from the get-go. The answer is that if the coach says something you feel is inappropriate, that's the time to get your parents, or other adults, involved. This doesn't mean you ask your parents to tell off your coach but rather that you let them know about the interaction and ask for their help and support.

Here's an example: "I tried to talk to the coach, but he said I was throwing a hissy fit. I don't want him to get even more frustrated with me, so do you think you could have a conversation with him? Maybe just ask why I'm on the bench, and what I can do to change that."

Give your parents all the information, not just the parts that make you look like an angel and your coach like the devil. If you did something wrong, fess up before they go to bat for you: "I know I've been late to a few practices, so that could be the reason, but I don't know." The more information they have, the better prepared they will be to approach him.

The Situation: I Need a Job

*I am applying for several jobs this summer and am starting
to get nervous about the interviews. I don't have much work
experience, and I don't really know what to expect. How can
I act confident in interviews and get my dream job?*

Even adults with lots of experience get nervous about job
interviews! It's hard to predict what kinds of questions you'll
be asked, and it's impossible to predict the personality of the
interviewer. Teens can be at a disadvantage, especially if they
don't have much or any experience with the interview process.
You know you need to "be prepared," but that doesn't mean
you know exactly what to do. You know you're supposed to act
"professional," but what does that mean?

Before You Say a Word

Making a good impression requires planning ahead, and that
includes dressing to impress. Even if the job is at a swimming
pool or a restaurant where the workers wear uniforms, what
you wear to the interview is important because it reflects your
attitude about the job. You want your future boss to view you as
more than just a student, so the clothes you wear to school probably won't cut it. Seek advice from a parent, teacher, counselor,
or mentor if you're not sure what's suitable for the particular
circumstances of your interview. In general, a nice pair of pants
and a conservative dress shirt will work fine. Go ahead and
express your individuality with jewelry and accessories, but

don't go overboard. The idea is to keep the interviewer's focus on what you're saying, not what you're wearing.

Be Prepared

At any job interview, you'll want to impress the interviewer from the moment you arrive. Don't just show up; come prepared. The more information you've prepped in advance, the better the impression you will make on the interviewer. For starters, bring the following with you to the interview:

* A copy of your application, even if they already have it.

* A list of references. Those important adults we talked about earlier come in handy sometimes. Call or e-mail to ask friends of the family, teachers, neighbors, or adults you have worked with who you think would speak highly of you to a prospective employer whether they would be willing to be a job reference for you.

* A résumé, if you have it. If not, make sure to ask the employer ahead of time if he or she needs one.

* Note pad and pen. Don't use your phone or a tablet to take notes; it's distracting and makes the interviewer wonder if you're texting. Take notes about important stuff, such as details about the job (the hours, the starting pay, and so on) or things you want to follow up on later.

 * Know your schedule. It's likely you'll be asked about your schedule. So know what days and hours you're available to work. Flexibility is definitely an asset because the more time you're available, the easier it is for the employer to set a work schedule. But don't overstate your availability, and don't commit to a schedule without being sure it will work. Also, know in advance how you would get to and from work.

Set the Scene

Arrive at the interview site a few minutes early. If you're not sure where to go, get directions ahead of time. If your mom and dad drive you to the interview, don't bring them in with you; ask them to wait in the car or at a nearby café. It's important to show up by yourself, speak for yourself, and connect with the interviewer without someone else's assistance.

Before you head inside, give yourself a little pep talk. Remind yourself what you're here for and why you are well qualified for the job. Build your self-confidence by giving yourself compliments: "You're really good with kids," "You've got great organization skills," "They'll be lucky to have you."

It's essential, of course, to use good manners when interviewing. Shake your interviewer's hand; make eye contact while talking; let the interviewer know you're mature, you know how to behave like an adult, and you're serious about wanting the job. Be polite, positive, and professional throughout the interview.

What to Say

This is where having a script really comes in handy. Hopefully, before you even get to the interview, you've done a little research on the company and you've practiced your answers to some typical interview questions. Make sure your answers are honest and at the same time give the interviewer a sense of what makes you the unique person you are. Here are some sample interview questions to get you started.

So tell me a little about yourself.

This is a where you talk about your interests in school and your hobbies outside of school. (Don't talk about social media or hanging out with friends unless it applies to the job you're interviewing for.) Here's a sample script for you to fill in and add to if you have more to say.

I'm in _____ grade at _____ (school). I'm really interested in _____ (subject) and hope to study it in college. Outside of school, I'm involved in _____ (sports team, clubs, or extracurricular activities). On the weekends I like to _____ (activities that interest you).

Why do you want a job right now? And why do you want to work here?

Don't just say it's about the cash. Explain what you hope to gain from working there. What skills will you be able to build by doing this work? What do you want to learn more about? What kinds of other jobs do you hope it might lead to? Why do you think you'll enjoy it?

Tell me about a challenging situation with a customer or someone you didn't see eye-to-eye with in the past. How did you handle it?

This one can be tough, so give yourself some time to think about it ahead of time and come up with a good answer. Be honest about the conflict or challenge you're describing and, at the same time, highlight the ways you were successful in resolving it and the things you learned from it.

Ask a few questions of your own. It shows the interviewer you're thoughtful, curious, and comfortable conversing with adults—a particularly good interview strategy if the position involves dealing directly with customers. Ask about how the business got started or what a typical day is like on the job. You could also ask: How is the schedule made? Are there opportunities to pick up more hours or take time off if you need to go out of town? How much notice is appropriate?

Remember to thank the person who interviewed you, both in person during the interview and later, with a note. If you have the person's e-mail address, send an e-mail thank-you note that day or the next. Otherwise, send a card in the mail, thanking the interviewer for taking the time to meet with you.

What to Do When...

What if the interview doesn't lead to a job offer? That can be really disappointing, especially if you were excited about the job. Make sure to thank the interviewer for giving you the chance to interview, and let him or her know you'd be interested in hearing about any opportunities that open up in the future. Try to be grateful for the practice you received with the interview because there will be another one at some point—maybe for a job you're even more excited about. In the meantime, keep trying to get clearer and clearer about your interests and the type of job you'd like to have. Don't be afraid to reach out to adults in your life who may be able to help point you in the right direction.

Been There, Done That—Advice from Women, and Girls, Who've Been in Your Shoes

Emily Roberts, MA, LPC, the Guidance Girl, is a psychotherapist, public speaker, and author.

My friends' parents often intimidated me when I was in high school. I thought if they didn't like me, then I would lose a friend. Instead of clamming up and being shy or spending time worrying about what they thought of me, I decided to put my confident communication skills to work. When I called, I'd use my manners. When I went to their house, I'd talk to them about school, ask them questions, and always help clean up or offer to. I was real and treated them like they were real people too, not parents on a pedestal. I was the friend that got invited on family vacations with them and that was even offered jobs. They saw that I was genuine and responsible. One summer, instead of serving slushies in the one-hundred degree weather like most of the kids my age, my friend's mom offered me a job at her office—big bucks and air conditioning, not to mention an awesome gig to put on my résumé. And I received a letter of recommendation for college. If you step up, use your manners, and don't shy away from conversations, adults will want to help you too.

195

Whatever you want to do in life, chances are, someone else has done exactly that. Instead of admiring—or envying—others' success from afar, why not be proactive and find a way to learn from the adults who are in a position to guide you? Remember, they can't help you if they don't hear you. The concluding chapter of this book isn't just a summary of everything we've gone over; it will also give you more ideas about making the most of your new communication skills.

Director's Note

People can't help you unless they can hear you.

#ExpressYourself

Conclusion:
The Assertive You

Don't dance around the perimeter of the person you want to be.
Step in fully and completely.

— Gabrielle Bernstein, *Miracles Now*

Congratulations! With lots of new skills under your belt, you're ready to take your place in the director's chair—well, almost. The tricky situations you've learned to handle are going to appear in real life soon (if they haven't already), so let's take the information you've gained off the pages and into your everyday conversations. Think of this section as the final rehearsal before you yell, "Action!" It's your chance to put the pieces together so you're ready to rock those assertive communication skills at any time.

Director's Note

Your words are powerful.
Be careful, kind, and above all else, confident.

#ExpressYourself

Exercise: Reassess Your Assertiveness

In the beginning of the book, you were asked to identify how comfortable you feel speaking up in typical teenage situations. Now it's time to reassess, meaning take a look at how much more confident you feel. Read the following scenarios and ask yourself how you think you would feel in each scenario and why. Choose one of these answers, and follow it with your explanation:

a) I would feel totally comfortable because…

b) I would feel somewhat uncomfortable because…

c) I would feel very nervous because…

If you want to take it a step further, write what you would say or do if you were in that situation.

Example: You're working on a class project, and it seems as if the leader is giving you all the work. How do you feel about confronting her?

I would feel totally comfortable because I would tell her that I feel nervous about getting it done on time and need her help. She will hear me because I'm not blaming her; I'm telling her my feelings.

1. You are confused about what your teacher is lecturing about. How do you feel about raising your hand to ask a question?

2. You have hours of homework, and your friend won't stop texting you about the drama she is dealing with. How do you feel about texting her back and saying that you're busy?

3. Your parents are blaming you for something your little sister did. How do you feel about telling them they're wrong?

4. You are at a party and don't know very many people. How do you feel about making conversation with someone new?

5. You are trying to study for your finals in the library. The students at the table next to you are being super loud. How do you feel about asking them to quiet down?

6. Your parents are making you stay home on a Saturday night because your grades have gone down, but there's an event you really want to attend. How do you feel about trying to negotiate a compromise?

7. Your teacher makes an inappropriate comment about you in front of the whole class. How do you feel about staying after class to talk to him about it?

8. You want to ask a crush to hang out after school. How do you feel about extending an invitation?

9. Your best friend keeps breaking plans with you to hang out with her boyfriend instead. How do you feel about telling her how disappointed you are (or that it's not okay with you that she keeps changing plans)?

10. A friend keeps posting photos of you that are embarrassing. How do you feel about asking her to take them down and to be more considerate of your feelings from now on?

What do you notice about your responses? Compare your responses now with the ones from the beginning of the book. Do you feel more confident in communicating with others? Which situations seem easier to deal with, and which ones still need some work? It's always a good idea to get in a confident frame of mind before heading into any situation, so how do you build yourself up before stepping on to the set? The next section will help you out.

Make Your Rights Your Reality

Remember the rights that were presented in chapters 2 through 7? It's time to turn those into your reality. Instead of just seeing the words on the page, you've got to really believe you are worthy of respect. A bad day or frustrating situation can set you up for some serious self-loathing! Instead of fading into the background and feeling sorry for yourself, read over your rights and put them in your phone or on your mirror to remind yourself about the things you deserve.

> *I used to get really sad and feel sorry for myself all the time. I hated feeling this way, so I started putting affirmations in my phone and decorating my bathroom mirror with phrases that reminded me of the person I wanted to be. Every day before lunch, the phrase "You are worth it. Stay strong!" pops up on my phone as a gentle reminder to not let anyone get me down. It totally helps me remember to focus on me, not the drama or the mean people in my life. —Lily, 17*

Surrounding yourself with powerful messages will help you embody the confident girl you want to become. Studies show the more you see it, the more you will believe it.

Go back to chapters 2 through 7 and find one or two rights that vibe with you. Write them down and follow the following steps to make them stick out in your mind.

Here's an example:

1. Identify your right: "You have the right to say no to anything that makes you feel uncomfortable." (chapter 6)

2. Why do you think you are worthy of this right, or why do you want to believe this? *Sometimes my friends make me feel guilty for saying no, and I feel bad about myself. I am in charge of my life, not my friends or my so-called friends. If I remember this, I will probably feel more confident when saying no to things that make me uncomfortable.*

3. Make it yours: take the "you" and any words that are in second person and turn them into first person. *I have the right to say no to anything that makes me uncomfortable.*

4. Make it even more powerful! Add in any phrase that makes you feel even more inspired. For example:

    I am worth it.

    I am strong.

    I've got this.

    I am confident.

    I am learning to be my best self.

    I am learning to trust myself.

    I deserve respect.

    I love myself.

    I am powerful.

    I rock.

Or add any phrase that makes you feel confident!

5. Rewrite your sentence again here or in your journal with your awesome add-on: *I have the right to say no to anything that makes me uncomfortable. I deserve respect.*

Now, say it out loud—seriously. It may sound silly, but when you hear it, you start to remember it more too! Say it to yourself in the mirror, or write it in your journal, on your screen saver, on the mirror (lipstick makes a great mirror marker!), on a sticky note next to your desk, or in your phone. The more you see your sentence, the more you really will believe it.

The Art of Improvisation

The scenarios presented throughout this book are accompanied by sample scripts to help guide you in these often-tricky situations. But sometimes, real life throws you unexpected challenges or moments that make your mind go blank. You won't always remember what you've learned, and you won't always know what to say. That's life—you can be prepared, but most things are pretty unpredictable. Still, however a situation goes, if you walk into it with real confidence, you can make it look as if you had it planned that way all along.

Often while making a movie, a director will ask the actors to improvise—to perform spontaneously, either loosely following a script or not following a script at all. If you've ever watched a comedy, chances are that some of the scenes were totally improvised—the director let the actors do their thing, and the audience had no idea it wasn't scripted. With improvisation, the actors are trusted to stay within some general boundaries, concepts, premises, or goals, rather than following a script word for word.

Improvising is an important skill in everyday life, as well. You may have a script in your mind for an important conversation, but that doesn't mean you'll remember all your lines when the time comes or that the other person will respond in the way you expected. And just as confidence is the key for actors, the same goes for you. So instead of trying to remember every single word, focus on the fact that you're more skilled and confident now than before you began this book. Even if you haven't practiced any of the skills yet, your brain has absorbed a lot. Heck, you just read a whole book about speaking up for yourself! So let your confidence be your guide. If you freeze up, chances are an idea will come to you shortly.

Director's Note

Sometimes you have to fake it before you make it.
Act the part even if you forget your lines.

#ExpressYourself

What Would You Do?

Here's a chance for you to practice improvisation. How would you handle the following situations without a script? Write what you would do or say in order to assert yourself, appear confident, and maintain your self-respect.

* You accidentally press send on your phone and realize you just sent your mom something that was intended for your crush! What do you say now?

* It's the first day of school, and you don't know anyone in your first-period class. You notice a friendly looking girl and sit next to her. How do you start a conversation?

* Your friend asks you to hold her pot at school because she's afraid her bag is going to get searched. What do you say?

* You're at your school's formal. When you go to use the bathroom, a bunch of seniors are in there taking shots, and they invite you to take one too. What do you do?

* You have to ask your boss for a few days off to go out of town with your parents. He is super strict about changing the schedule. How do you approach it with him?

There really is no one right answer in each of those situations—or for that matter, in any social situation. So remember, this is *your* movie, and you get to decide how you want the story to turn out. With some new skills and a little practice in your pocket, you'll be much more ready to take the lead.

Want more? The next section lists other resources that will motivate and inspire you.

The director's chair is waiting for you. Speak up, stay strong, and know that when you express yourself, you respect yourself!

Director's Note

You are the director of your own life.
Don't let others steal the spotlight.

#ExpressYourself

Resources

Inspiration

Gabrielle Bernstein
http://www.gabbyb.tv
Twitter: @GabbyBernstein
Instagram: @GabbyBernstein
Facebook: http://www.facebook.com/gabriellebernstein
Social Network: http://www.herfuture.com
App: Spirit Junkie
Book: *Miracles Now*

Nitika Chopra
http://www.yourbellalife.com
Twitter: @YourBellaLife
Instagram: @nitikachopra
Facebook: http://www.facebook.com/BellaNitikaChopra

Lena Dunham

http://lenadunham.com/
Twitter: @lenadunham
Instagram: @lenadunham
Book: *Not That Kind of Girl*

Tavi Gevinson

http://www.rookiemag.com
Twitter: @tavitulle
Instagram: @tavitulle
Facebook: https://www.facebook.com/RookieMag

Emily Greener

http://www.iamthatgirl.com
Twitter: @iamthatgirl, @thatgirlgreener
Instagram: @iamthatgirl, @thatgirlgreener
http://www.facebook.com/BeThatGirl

Alexis Jones

http://www.iamthatgirl.com
Twitter: @iamthatgirl, @missalexisjones
Instagram: @iamthatgirl @missalexisjones
http://www.facebook.com/BeThatGirl
Book: *I Am That Girl: How to Speak Your Truth, Discover Your Purpose, and #bethatgirl*

Mindy Kaling

http://theconcernsofmindykaling.com/
Instagram: @mindykaling
Twitter: @mindykaling

Facebook: http://www.facebook.com/OfficialMindyKaling
Book: *Is Everyone Hanging Out Without Me? (And Other Concerns)*

Ruby Karp
http://hellogiggles.com/author/ruby-karp
Twitter: @RubyKarp
Instagram: @RubyKarp

Haley Kilpatric
http://www.mygirltalk.org
Twitter: @girltalkinc
Instagram: @girltalkinc
Facebook: http://www.facebook.com/InspireGirlTalk
Book: *The Drama Years*

Danielle LaPorte
http://www.daniellelaporte.com
Twitter: @daniellelaporte
Instagram: @daniellelaporte
Facebook: http://www.facebook.com/Danielle.LaPorte.Inc
App: Conversation Starters

Emily Roberts MA, LPC
http://www.theguidancegirl.com
Twitter: @guidancegirlem
Instagram: @guidancegirlem
Facebook: http://www.facebook.com/TheGuidanceGirl

Marianne Williamson

http://www.marianne.com/

Facebook: http://www.facebook.com/williamsonmarianne

Twitter: @marwilliamson

Instagram: @mariannewilliamson

Apps: Miracle Cards, A Year of Daily Wisdom

Alexis Wolfer

http://www.thebeautybean.com

Twitter: @alexiswolfer, @thebeautybean

Instagram: @alexiswolfer, @thebeautybean

Facebook: http://www.facebook.com/TheBeautyBean

Other Awesome Organizations By Girls and For Girls

Amy Poehler's Smart Girls at the Party, http://amysmartgirls.com

Beauty Redefined, http://www.beautyredefined.net/

Dove Self-Esteem Campaign, http://selfesteem.dove.us

Gurl.com, http://www.gurl.com

Girls for a Change, http://www.girlsforachange.org

HelloGiggles, http://hellogiggles.com

Spark Movement, http://www.sparksummit.com/

Team Bullied, http://teambullied.com

Mental Health

Crisis Call Center, 800-273-8255 or text ANSWER to 839863, http://crisiscallcenter.org/crisisservices.html

CyberTipline (for suspected sexual abuse or exploitation), 800-843-5678, http://www.cybertipline.com

Love Is Respect, National Teen Dating Abuse Helpline, 866-331-9474, http://www.loveisrespect.org

National Hopeline Network, 800-442-HOPE (4673), http://www.hopeline.com

National Eating Disorders Association, 800-931-2237, http://www.nationaleatingdisorders.org

National Domestic Violence Hotline, 800-799-SAFE (7233), http://www.thehotline.org

National Mental Health Association Hotline, (twenty-four hours a day, seven days a week) 800-273-TALK (8255), http://www.mentalhealthamerica.net/

National Suicide Hotline, 800-SUICIDE (784-2433), http://www.suicidepreventionlifeline.org

National Suicide Prevention Lifeline, 800-273-TALK (8255), http://www.suicidepreventionlifeline.org

The Trevor Lifeline (available only in the United States), 866-4-U-TREVOR (488-7386), http://www.thetrevorproject.org

Emily Roberts, MA, LPC, is a psychotherapist, parenting consultant, educational speaker, and author. She created *The Guidance Girl* brand to help empower and educate girls on how to feel confident, build self-esteem, and develop communication skills. Roberts is aware of the challenges faced by both teens and women, and has built a practice by positioning herself as a therapeutic mentor and consultant. She is an intensively trained dialectical behavior therapist and leads groups for young adults in New York City at Hartstein Psychological Services. She is a guest contributor for *Dr. Drew On Call* on HLN, and speaks about mental health and self-esteem in the media. As a contributing author for HealthyPlace.com, Roberts writes the weekly blog *Building Self-Esteem* and is also a parenting consultant and blogger for the Neurogistics Corporation. Roberts is cofounder of The Talking Room—a workshop program in Austin, TX, that helps girls ages five to eleven develop self-esteem, confidence, leadership, friendship skills, and teaches stress reduction activities with an emphasis on creating healthy boundaries with others and through technology.

Foreword writer **Jennifer L. Hartstein, PsyD,** is the owner of Hartstein Psychological Services, a group psychotherapy practice in New York, NY. Hartstein works with children, adolescents, and families with a wide range of psychological diagnoses, and specializes in the treatment of high-risk children and adolescents. She has received intensive training in adolescent suicide assessment, and has specialized in this population for several years, using a variety of treatment approaches, including dialectical behavior therapy (DBT). She is on the advisory board for MTV's *A Thin Line,* which focuses on the digital behaviors of today's young people. Additionally, she is a psychological contributor for NBC's *Today Show,* as well as other national news outlets. Hartstein is author of *Princess Recovery: A How-To Guide to Raising Strong, Empowered Girls Who Can Create Their Own Happily Ever Afters.*

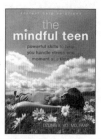